PRAISE FOR *GIVE HOSPITALITY*

"*Give Hospitality* serves as a powerful tool for all leaders who strive to make the workplace a more connected and understanding environment. Taylor is a talented student of leadership and does an extraordinary job showing how far generosity can get you."

—Ken Potrock, President, Major Events
Integration, The Walt Disney Company

"Taylor does a wonderful job capturing the foundational elements of great hospitality—culture, mutual respect, and teamwork—in an informative, compelling, and entertaining format that showcases his deep understanding of our industry. This is a great read for anyone entering a career in hospitality, or for those looking for a beautiful reminder of what makes this industry so special."

—Scott Taber, Senior Vice President, Global
Hospitality, Four Seasons Hotels and Resorts

"Taylor provides clear direction and tools to create deep connections across a team. By using this road map, which is rooted in simple yet meaningful conversations, a culture of hospitality can be fostered in any team, in any industry and the results are bound to translate to the employee and customer experience."

—Abigail Charpentier, Senior Vice President and
Chief Human Resources Officer, Aramark

"This story not only captures the magic of the Aloha Spirit, but it also GIVEs all of us a road map for how to inspire others to deliver heartfelt, memorable hospitality to our guests, customers, clients, and especially to the people we lead."

—Scott Amasio, Director of Sales, Disney Vacation Club

"Taylor's writing reminds leaders and teams to learn from negative experiences in our past while looking to the future with inspiration and optimism. This book has a magical way of teaching lessons for how to live and work generously, while feeling like you're on the beach having a conversation with a friend."

—Amy Svendsen, Director of Sales and Marketing
Compensation, Hilton Grand Vacations

"Our leadership retreat with Taylor was a hit. He brings a unique blend of fun, passion, comprehensive knowledge, and Edutainment to sessions in real life just as he conveys in this book. True to Taylor's style, the *Give Hospitality* story is entertaining, inspiring, and provides an actionable guide for any leader in any industry to create a culture of generous hospitality on their team."

—Erik Palmer, Vice President of Operations, Highgate Hotels—New York

"Over the years, I've seen Taylor transform teams by helping leaders understand the power of emotional connections, meaningful recognition, and instilling a shared sense of purpose. His approach to Coaching with Grace, Grit, and Intention teaches leaders to strike a balance between compassion and determination, guiding their teams to overcome challenges with strength and intentionality. Taylor doesn't just focus on results—he focuses on the people behind those results, helping them grow and thrive. *Give Hospitality* and the story of Summer Grace and Kauwela Resorts paints a perfect picture of what the magic of generosity and hospitality will do for any culture, in any industry."

—Kimberly Isely-Pesto, Senior Manager, Training
Delivery Strategy and Execution, United Airlines

"In *Give Hospitality* Taylor Scott truly embodies the transformative power of kindness, compassion, and leadership in the workplace. Through engaging storytelling and practical insights, Taylor demonstrates how a culture of generosity and hospitality can elevate both employee satisfaction and guest experiences. This inspiring read is a blueprint for leaders seeking to create meaningful work environments and deliver exceptional service. I had the pleasure of collaborating with Taylor on a client engagement and witnessed firsthand how his inspiring approach motivated the team to strive for excellence, both personally and collectively."

—Joanna Dissin, Director, Workplace Experience, Jones Lang Lasalle

"I've had the pleasure of working with Taylor over the years as well as enjoying his previous books. This is the best example yet of him sharing his experiences of giving hospitality. The book contains activities easy to consume and practice while providing the reader rich stories transferable across every industry."

—Chris Arnett, Senior Director, Brand Standards and Compliance Strategy, Choice Hotels International

"If you're seeking to elevate your leadership and inspire your team, *Give Hospitality* is an important read. Taylor Scott offers a unique leadership onboarding process that encourages self-reflection and actionable growth. In an era of toxic workplaces, his fresh perspective provides a positive model for effective and authentic leadership."

—Alexander Koch, Global Vice President, The Cornell Hotel Society

"*Give Hospitality* is the book you need to reaffirm your passion for the hospitality industry! It is an inspiring and easy read for individuals and teams who want to create inclusive and unforgettable experiences for guests."

—Mia J. Blom, HBCU Hospitality Lecturer

"Seasoned leaders and emerging leaders alike will find this uplifting story relatable and incredibly actionable. For leaders looking to create a positive, inclusive, and hospitality-centric culture, this inspiring story is the perfect guide for all of us."

—Amber Moshakos, President, LM Restaurants

"Our team has laughed more, smiled, been more engaged, and we're definitely feeling more fulfilled at work since using the actionable applications Taylor provides in this book. I have found his books and energy to be very encouraging in this challenging time in healthcare."

—Laura Hagley, Senior Director of Quality, Dartmouth Health

"The story of Summer Grace and Kauwela Resorts reminds all of us that we're more alike than we are different. Whether you're a leader of people, a member of a team, or an educator, on any level, this book—the timeless leadership principles, the story, and especially the very relevant and practical applications—will help all of us create a more inclusive world at work, at home, and in the communities we serve."

—Joseph E. Hochreiter, Superintendent of Schools,
City School District of Albany, NY

GIVE
HOSPITALITY

Also by Taylor Scott

Lead with Hospitality
Ballgames to Boardrooms

GIVE
HOSPITALITY

A Hopeful Story of What Happens When We Live, Work, and Love from a Place of Generosity

TAYLOR SCOTT

Matt Holt Books
An Imprint of BenBella Books, Inc.
Dallas, TX

Matt Holt is an imprint of BenBella Books, Inc.
8080 N. Central Expressway
Suite 1700
Dallas, TX 75206
benbellabooks.com
Send feedback to feedback@benbellabooks.com

BenBella and *Matt Holt* are federally registered trademarks.

Printed in the United States of America
10 9 8 7 6 5 4 3 2 1

Library of Congress Control Number: 2024058381
ISBN 978-1-63774-700-1 (hardcover)
ISBN 978-1-63774-701-8 (electronic)

Editing by Katie Dickman
Copyediting by Michael Fedison
Proofreading by Jenny Bridges and Denise Pangia
Text design and composition by Aaron Edmiston
Cover design by Brigid Pearson
Printed by Lake Book Manufacturing

Special discounts for bulk sales are available.
Please contact bulkorders@benbellabooks.com.

For Arthur.

For Maui.

For the Hospitality Industry.

CONTENTS

DAY THREE

DAY FOUR

DAY FIVE

ALOHA

Summer Grace intentionally left a job that started off as a great experience but over time deteriorated as the organization's toxicity revealed itself repeatedly. Her former leader made her feel less than and, in a word, uncomfortable. She was recently invited to join Kauwela Resorts* in a leadership role as a front desk manager, but she was weighing her options before accepting.

Summer Grace has always had an appreciation for hospitality, travel, and tourism experiences. Growing up, some of her fondest memories and most magical moments with family and friends were times spent together at restaurants, hotels, and resorts on short but memorable vacations.

Summer Grace was in her mid-thirties, and for her entire professional career she'd received feedback that she always presented herself with grace, class, and just the right amount of passionate, spunky fire, which tended to elevate others around her and keep her own leaders on their toes. She had grown to love and appreciate that feedback and leaned into carrying herself with both *grace* and *grit*. She was always *that person* who had friends from all different races and places, and she

---

* *Kauwela* (pronounced KAH-oo WEH-luh) means "summer" in Hawaiian.

tended to be *that person* others could turn to for advice, encouragement, or just a genuine good time. She loved fashion, music, basketball, reading all types of books, staying as physically fit as possible, and she loved a good happy hour moment at a hotel lobby bar or restaurant. Growing up the eldest of four siblings, she was a natural leader, having honed her leadership skills much earlier in life than most as she often was left in charge when both of her parents traveled frequently for work. She was as beautiful on the outside as she was on the inside. She wasn't always confident growing up, but in this season of transition, she felt like she was finally coming into her own. She knew who she was, and for the first time, she knew who she wanted to further blossom into—personally and professionally.

While she still had no idea what the word *Kauwela* meant just yet, Summer Grace was considering Kauwela Resorts for several reasons. Stories of Kauwela Resorts have long been told in trade magazines, books, articles, and through their inspiring ads and commercials. Summer Grace followed Kauwela Resorts on social media, experienced a couple of their properties during a few amazing long weekends with her friends and family members, and connected to the brand on an emotional level because of the memories she'd made over the years. Every experience and every story, whether it was a simple cup of coffee, a cocktail experience at the lobby bar, a long weekend hotel stay, or simply a brief sizzle reel on a Kauwela Resorts commercial, always left Summer Grace feeling happy.

As she weighed options for her next career move, Summer Grace and a group of her closest girlfriends booked a trip to the Kauwela Resorts property that offered her a job. Before signing her offer letter, she wanted to experience it firsthand to see if she felt the magic.

Though it would be a fun trip, she was nervous and arrived at the airport early to make sure her TSA PreCheck was intact before braving the security checkpoint line. For some reason it wasn't populating on her boarding pass when she checked in on her airline app.

The customer service representative at the counter settled those nerves right away, resolving the issue with a simple fix in what Summer Grace thought was a very pleasant interaction. An hour or so later, she was on board her flight and settling into "Long Weekend Mode."

As soon as the flight attendants made their first appearance with the beverage cart, Summer Grace thought, *Why not get things started off with a mai tai.* After all, she knew Kauwela Resorts celebrated Hawaiian culture, so she wanted to get in the spirit. With each sip, she was getting more excited to reconnect with her best friends. Beginning to daydream about the afternoon she'd have at the pool, she noticed the beverage napkin read "*Mālama.*"

Her favorite airline was known for their many routes to and from the Hawaiian Islands. This could be a sign, she thought. As she read the napkin, she learned the meaning of *mālama* in Hawaiian—"to care for." It was the airline's way of welcoming their guests and passengers while also sharing the story of how they're committed to the rebuilding efforts on Maui after the tragic fires decimated the beloved harbor town of Lahaina. Summer Grace visited the website link listed on the napkin and after reading stories about the widespread generosity and outpouring of love for Maui, she donated right then and there, at 35,000 feet. It just felt like the right thing to do.

ALOHA IS MORE THAN A WARM GREETING

During her three-day-long weekend at Kauwela Resorts with her girlfriends, Summer Grace was inspired by the beauty of the Aloha Spirit. She could see and feel it in every interaction with the Kauwela Resorts team. While at the resort, she not only learned about the storied history of the Hawaiian Islands, but also just how powerful the Spirit of Aloha really is.

She was especially inspired by a series of interactions that organically turned into a full-blown friendship with a bartender from Maui's historic harbor town of Lahaina. Pua was her name, and she always had a beautiful yellow hibiscus flower tucked perfectly behind her right ear. She engaged Summer Grace and her girlfriends in amazing conversations in the most unassuming, yet magical, way. Their multiple lobby bar experiences were the best part of the trip, with the view of the sun setting over the Pacific Ocean and perhaps the most beautiful, yet subtle flower arrangement on their table, which seemed to lift everyone's spirits each evening.

Through conversations each night, Summer Grace and her friends learned from Pua the true meaning of *Aloha*.

They learned this magical word meant more than just a warm greeting.

The more Pua shared, the more curious and inquisitive Summer Grace and her girlfriends became. Pua told them powerful stories that had been passed down for decades in her hometown of Lahaina, on Maui, Hawaii's "Valley Isle." Before Pua left for the evening on their last night, she brought Summer Grace and her friends a square card, slightly larger than a postcard, which explained more about the *Spirit of Aloha*.

Pua was as great of a conversationalist as she was a mixologist. When she shared that the *Spirit of Aloha* was at the core of everything they do at Kauwela Resorts, Summer Grace knew she wanted to be a part of it. Staring at the fresh flowers on the table, with the sunset in the distance, she reflected on the values of *kindness, compassion, encouragement, hospitality*, and *leadership*.

Those values resonated with her because each of them reflected who she wanted to become in her life and career. She'd always found a sense of purpose being the person to lift the spirits of others, like beautiful flowers light up an otherwise gloomy day.

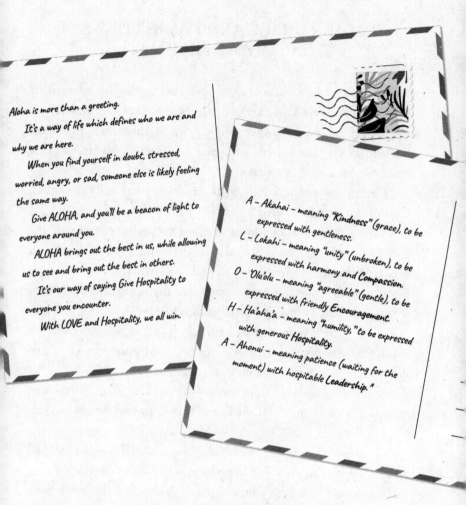

Aloha is more than a greeting.

It's a way of life which defines who we are and why we are here.

When you find yourself in doubt, stressed, worried, angry, or sad, someone else is likely feeling the same way.

Give ALOHA, and you'll be a beacon of light to everyone around you.

ALOHA brings out the best in us, while allowing us to see and bring out the best in others.

It's our way of saying Give Hospitality to everyone you encounter.

With LOVE and Hospitality, we all win.

A – Akahai – meaning "Kindness" (grace), to be expressed with gentleness.

L – Lokahi – meaning "unity" (unbroken), to be expressed with harmony and Compassion.

O – 'Olu'olu – meaning "agreeable" (gentle), to be expressed with friendly Encouragement.

H – Ha'aha'a – meaning "humility," to be expressed with generous Hospitality.

A – Ahonui – meaning patience (waiting for the moment) with hospitable Leadership. *

Since her personal values aligned with those of Kauwela Resorts, she made the decision to join the team as a front desk manager. When she returned home after her insightful and inspiring trip, she signed her offer letter and began preparations to start her new job, hoping this one would be better than the last.

* "Hawai'i Law of the Aloha Spirit," https://www.hawaii.edu/uhwo/clear/home/lawaloha.html.

SUMMER GRACE AND PUA RECONNECT, THIS TIME AS TEAMMATES

When Summer Grace first walked back into the lobby to begin her journey at Kauwela Resorts, the first person she saw was Pua. As the two locked eyes from across the lobby, genuine smiles on both of their faces lit up the room as Pua welcomed her former guest turned new teammate back to the property.

On her way to check into the hotel for her two-week orientation, Summer Grace reconnected with Pua.

"Thank you so much for the gracious hospitality you showed my girlfriends and me when we stayed here last month. I've been in a rough season of transition, unsure of what to do or where to go next with my career, and the conversations we had lifted my spirits and brightened what would have been a gloomy three days filled with self-doubt. I love flowers in every season—good, bad, ugly—and each night when we spent time with you in the lobby bar, you brightened my spirits just like flowers always cheer me up when I'm down."

Summer Grace was a little uncomfortable being that vulnerable so early in her experience, but she leaned into it anyway. Somehow, this just felt right.

With her warm smile, Pua replied, "Aw, well, I'm so glad you had an uplifting stay with us, and I heard you were joining our team! I'm so excited to work alongside you, and please don't be a stranger. I'm here for you as you transition. So, anything you need or if you have any questions, you know where to find me."

Pua was just as warm and uplifting in that moment as Summer Grace remembered from their prior interactions on her long weekend trip. This time, they were teammates!

"One more question that I forgot to ask: What does your name— Pua—mean in the Hawaiian culture?" Summer Grace asked.

"Flower," Pua said, with her usual grin stretching from ear to ear.

With a lump in her throat and tears welling up, Summer Grace smiled right back, and said, "Yep. That makes perfect sense. I'll see you later, I'm sure. Thank you again."

While she was still a bit nervous to begin her new career at Kauwela Resorts, the short yet impactful conversation made her feel welcomed and more comfortable. She couldn't help but notice these subtle signs—*mālama*, and the story of its meaning on the napkin that inspired her to donate; her mai tai that seemed to put her on island time; and now Pua's name meaning "flower."

As she walked to the front desk to check in, she smiled.

SUMMER GRACE'S WEEK ONE EXPERIENCE AT KAUWELA RESORTS

Kauwela Resorts was committed to creating meaningful experiences for guests and employees alike. Creating memorable experiences guides everything they do, including how they welcome newly hired leaders and team members into their community. Summer Grace's first two weeks on the job were quite different from anywhere she'd worked in the past. Rather than sifting through a mountain of paperwork like the last time she started a new job, Summer Grace's experience started with a series of conversations and actual experiences in various parts of one of the brand's hotels. Most importantly, she connected on a personal level with other people starting in their new roles with Kauwela Resorts.

Shopping, dining, recreational activities at the resort, cocktails at the lobby bar with Pua, and meals every single day in their signature restaurant, Gracious Café, filled her mornings, afternoons, and most evenings of Week One.

Her only task was to simply *experience* the Kauwela Resorts vibe that so many guests and employees had grown to love and share stories about time and again.

Each day, Summer Grace returned to her guest room filled with hope for what she knew would be a fulfilling journey—being a part of the Kauwela Resorts leadership team. It felt so refreshing given how toxic and negative her most recent employer was. Midway through that first week, she caught herself in a state of wonder as she could almost *feel the Aloha.*

What is it about this place, she contemplated, *that fills people up with so much happiness and hope? Is it the beauty of the property? Is it the tasty food, the refreshing cocktails with a view, or the layout of the lobby, so open, welcoming, and inviting?*

She couldn't quite put her finger on just one thing that made the experience so uplifting. Her favorite part of the day was the end of each night, hopping into the freshly made bed that only great hotels seemingly know how to make so comfortable. On the final night of Week One, she'd get a solid night's rest before starting Week Two of her new job.

SUMMER GRACE IS CURIOUS, EXCITED, AND NERVOUS ALL AT ONCE

Week Two began with a one-on-one conversation with Arthur, her general manager and new boss. Arthur lit up every single room he entered with his presence. That was one reason every new hire orientation for leaders joining Kauwela Resorts took part in the two-week immersion at Arthur's property. It was by design, as the corporate office loved the way Arthur and his team welcomed new team members into the Kauwela Resorts family.

Right away, Summer Grace noticed that his smile was visibly genuine. It was glaringly obvious that the smile everyone saw on his face was connected directly to the love in his heart. He was just one of those people, Summer Grace thought to herself, who always seemed to bring out the best in others.

She had so many questions for Arthur, who had been a hotel general manager most of his professional life. She wondered how he'd been able to navigate his journey as a person of color, often in the minority in the industry. As a person of color herself, a Black female from Illinois, Summer Grace's personal and professional experiences had been full of ups and downs. She thought Arthur had to have experienced similar feelings and emotions along the way. As curious as she'd ever been, and with nervous yet excited anticipation, Summer Grace was looking forward to learning how Arthur had been so successful in his career despite the challenges.

SUMMER GRACE MEETS ARTHUR IN THE HOTEL LOBBY

Summer Grace's nervous anticipation heading into Week Two dropped a few levels as soon as she saw Arthur walking toward her from across the lobby. He'd wave to children and adults, team members and guests, and it was like the opening scene of a musical at Richard Rodgers Theatre on Broadway, as he charismatically picked up the lone piece of trash on the ground along the way while simultaneously making everyone in his midst feel special.

He seemed to glide across the lobby.

"Aloha, Summer Grace! How was Week One?" Arthur greeted with equal parts enthusiasm and hospitality. There he went, yet again, with that presence.

"Good morning, Arthur," Summer Grace replied with an enthusiastic smile to match her general manager's. "Well, it was just so very cool. Everything was great, from the food to my hotel room to my time spent with others in my incoming new-hire class at the pool. But what keeps me engaged and filled up with so much excitement for this new job is the way all your team members treat people. I found myself just sitting back, watching and listening. I have so many questions for you! How do you do that? How on earth are you able to get all these people—Black people, Latina people, Latino people, Asian people, Asian American people, White people, indigenous people, LGBTQ+ people, island people, and team members from all these different generations—to get along so well, let alone create such memorable experiences for your guests?"

"You're very observant, my friend, and that's one of the many reasons I invited you to come work with us. I get those same questions almost every day, from our guests as well as analysts, scholars, and consulting firms wanting to know our secrets. The reality is, it's not just one thing, or even a few things. Instead, it's hundreds of little things we not only do, but share with each other in our everyday conversations. So, rather than give you a boring lecture today, I'm going to walk you down to the Aloha Conference Room, where you'll spend most of your time this week."

"Okay, great. What exactly am I doing the rest of the time here in Week Two? I've already experienced all of Kauwela Resorts' atmosphere, drinks, shopping, dining, and recreational activities. What else is there to experience?" Summer Grace respectfully asked.

"You want to know how we pull this stuff off, don't you?" Arthur playfully engaged. "After all, you'll soon be one of our most visible leaders at our most popular property to lead all this magic we create every day."

"Well, of course, but that just seems like a lot of conversations," Summer Grace replied with an inquisitive tone, which Arthur knew would eventually be quenched in her Week Two *experience*.

ARTHUR WALKS SUMMER GRACE TO THE ALOHA CONFERENCE ROOM TO MEET ARLENE AND NICK

"I'm taking you to the Aloha Conference Room where you'll meet Arlene and Nick. They're my friends who I met many years ago. They created a brand called Lead with Hospitality, LLC years ago, which inspired me so much when I first met them that I wanted to work with them to further the Kauwela Resorts mission and cause. We've been partners ever since.

"The Kauwela Resorts purpose is: *To inspire selflessness, generosity, and hearts for hospitality so that jobs are transformed into truly meaningful work in a place where guests can relax, recharge, and reconnect over conversations about the things that matter.*

"They have creative ways of teaching and inspiring, which they call *Edutainment.* I think you'll really enjoy the conversations. You'll connect with your new colleagues and teammates in a genuine and authentic way, which I believe will be right up your alley."

Arthur's whole demeanor changed, as if it could get any more positive, when he talked about Lead with Hospitality, LLC. "Their values aligned with my personal values and our Kauwela Resorts values, so we really connected on a human level. Their values are to *connect, serve, engage,* and *inspire,* in that order. We lean into our partnership with them and their like-minded approach to how we live, work, and love, as a reminder to take the focus off ourselves and redirect it, spreading love and *Aloha* to others. We adopted the Lead with Hospitality philosophy years ago around here, and it worked wonders for our culture, which continues to serve us and those we serve very well.

"We make it all about giving the best of ourselves to others, whether it's fellow members of our team or our guests. It's simple, but not always easy to deliver. However, we've found that at our very core, though we may look different on the outside, we're all human beings with a need for relationship and good, old-fashioned community on the inside.

"Kauwela Resorts is what it is, and means so much to those who work here and play here because of one underlying thread woven intricately into everything we say and do. **It's about generosity—living, working, and even *loving* from a place of generosity in our hearts. It's our way of saying, *Give Hospitality to everyone you encounter*.**"

Arthur gave Summer Grace just enough to pique her curiosity but stopped himself right there. He didn't want to take away from the magic of what brings any Lead with Hospitality, LLC experience to life, which are the conversations with people about the things that matter.

"So that's it? Just a cool brand with an *Edutainment* style of facilitating conversations? That's how you pull off all this magic and get people to treat each other so well?" Summer Grace was perplexed, and she wanted to know more.

Arthur laughed, almost as if he knew just how much Summer Grace's experience was about to be elevated.

"Experiences are nothing more than stories told through acts of service, inspiring words, and, most importantly, the feelings we feel. So, we bring our very own culture of *gracious hospitality* to life and set out to inspire others to do the same with what we call Hospitality Conversations. That's what you'll do in Week Two, every day this week, with Arlene and Nick."

"Got it. But what can we possibly talk about all day, every day?" Summer Grace giggled as she asked.

"You'd be surprised," Arthur said as he opened the door to the Aloha Conference Room, where Arlene and Nick welcomed them both.

DAY ONE

Chapter 1

GIVE Compassion

Nick, like Arthur, was larger than life, inside and out. Standing six feet, four inches tall, he certainly had a presence—a positive one. As tall as Nick was in stature, Summer Grace couldn't help but notice his personality seemed to exude the very messages of generosity and self-lessness that were the foundations of the Lead with Hospitality, LLC brand.

NICK WELCOMES SUMMER GRACE TO HOSPITALITY CONVERSATIONS

"ALOHA! Welcome to Hospitality Conversations, Week Two of the rest of your career," Nick said with a heartfelt, genuine smile. "We're so glad you made the decision to join Kauwela Resorts. Arthur filled us in on your story, having dealt with a toxic culture in your last job with your former leader. It's different here. You're now in a place where it's okay to not be okay. We just believe we don't have to stay that way. Our secret, which isn't really a secret, is to simply lean into engaging, meaningful conversations with our coworkers, leaders, and especially our guests every chance we get. So, welcome. Make yourself at home, grab some water, coffee, or tea, and we'll get started in a few minutes."

Summer Grace's nerves had already been calmed by her short, yet impactful, conversation with Pua, followed by her walk and talk with Arthur. Now, with Nick's warm welcome into the Hospitality Conversations experience, she took another calming breath and said, "Thank you—so much—for the welcome. Since last week I've had a gut feeling that I've somehow landed exactly where I'm supposed to be. I'm very excited to be here."

SUMMER GRACE NOTICES DIFFERENCES THAT MATTER

She looked around the room, and while some were already engaged in conversations, several people were keeping to themselves. *This is interesting*, she thought. For the first time in her professional career, as she looked around the room, there were just as many people who looked like her, a person of color, as there were White people. As Summer Grace grabbed a bottle of water and found a seat, she also noticed something else. There were just as many, if not more, females as males in the room.

This was different than her last job; the diversity in ethnicities, gender, age, and even how people were dressed brought a certain positive energy and buzz to the room.

Summer Grace smiled to herself, got situated, and said hello to her new coworkers at her table.

ARLENE KICKS OFF HOSPITALITY CONVERSATIONS

Arlene, with a magnetically attractive presence and personality of her own, greeted everyone with the same genuine, authentic smile Summer Grace had noticed on most of the faces working at Kauwela Resorts.

"Aloha and welcome to Day One of Hospitality Conversations! We'll have plenty of time to get to know one another because the culture here at Kauwela Resorts is to simply engage, engage, and engage some more in meaningful conversations. That's what we'll do all week long. Are we ready to get started?"

Everyone nodded and answered verbally with a resounding, "YES."

Arlene and Nick were both former educators with years of experience preparing students, school systems, and the next generation of leaders. They knew how to engage an audience and create environments conducive for collaboration and learning. *Edutainment*, to them, was a calling, and more than simply a passion. Both former athletes, they brought the same level of enthusiasm to setting up the room as they did in how they delivered their content. Tables were preset with Participant Guides, name tents, ink pens, and even snacks neatly placed as centerpieces in the middle of each six-top round table.

As Arlene eloquently unpacked the Day One objectives, Summer Grace looked around the room. Others were also looking around with smiles, winks, and what seemed to be an overwhelming sense that Kauwela Resorts would absolutely, positively be a welcome change from what they'd all experienced in their former places of employment up to that point.

JUST LIKE THAT, WEEK TWO IS UNDERWAY

"What does the word *compassion* mean to you?" Arlene threw out the first question of the experience. "Summer Grace, how about you? What does *compassion* mean to you?"

"Well, I've always thought of compassion as simply showing other people you care about them," Summer Grace said, diving right into the conversation.

"I agree. It's recognizing when others might need help," AJ, Summer Grace's new coworker and fellow front desk manager, enthusiastically shared. AJ had spent the last few years working in boutique hotels in Miami, on South Beach. He was born in New York City, but grew up in Southern California, and had earned his undergraduate degree in hotel and resort management. He had a laid-back "SoCal demeanor" about him. However, when it came to anything hotel or hospitality related, he was dialed in and obsessed! Summer Grace loved his vibe and the two had already bonded during Week One over their shared love of craft cocktails and happy hour appetizers by the pool. "And you know what? On my flight on the way here, the word *mālama* was on a beverage napkin!" AJ said. "It means 'to care for' in Hawaiian. Is that a thing here?"

"I saw that, too, on my flight! I loved it and immediately went to that website and donated money to rebuild Maui. After reading about what happened to Lahaina with the fires, I just had to do it," Summer Grace replied, surprising herself with how outgoing she was being right out of the gate, but she just felt so comfortable in this environment for some reason.

"Absolutely. Compassion is going out of your way to help people: cheering them up when they're sad, physically helping them if they're hurt, and lifting them up with your positivity. And yes, *mālama* is a total thing here!" Arlene continued. "Compassion means to recognize when other people may need some help. It's lifting them up with our positivity, making them laugh again. It's *mālama* all day, every day around here."

Everyone was nodding along with Arlene's every word.

"Why is *giving compassion* important, as a leader?" Arlene threw out another question for the group.

Amber, the new food and beverage director, chimed in, "When we *Give Compassion*, we help people *feel* better about themselves and better about their lives. Also, when we show we care about people, *giving* them *compassion*, as you call it, it's good for our own mental and physical health; not to mention, it helps the other person's mental health (their attitude) and physical health as well."

Amber was clearly wise beyond her years; she had grown up with amazing mentors at home and in her career working in restaurants throughout her entire professional life. Born and raised in the Carolinas, Amber appeared to be in her late 40s, and when she spoke, everyone physically turned their heads to get the full experience. She was equal parts wise and warm, both inviting and direct. Summer Grace knew right then and there she wanted to learn more from Amber. *That's how I want to be one day*, she thought.

Arlene loved the participation and early energy. "Yes! Compassion really is a powerful thing. That's why it's our most foundational value here at Kauwela Resorts. Many of you may already be aware, but here are the reasons *compassion* is so core to who we are and who we want to continually strive to become, individually and collectively, as a team." Arlene was a natural teacher, but she embodied a little extra flair, which kept everyone entertained. She took pride in what she called *Edutainment*, which was to create an environment for learning in entertaining and memorable ways.

The energy in the room was palpable, positive, and productive.

ARLENE UNPACKS WHAT THE SCIENCE SAYS ABOUT COMPASSION

Arlene began unpacking what the research says about compassion, while projecting a list of key takeaways on the screen at the front of the room.

Giving Compassion Makes Us Happy: Research has shown that we experience just as much pleasure and joy when we observe someone giving charitable donations or when we, ourselves, give of ourselves—our time, talent, or resources—as when we eat our favorite foods or even when we receive large sums of money!

Giving Compassion Makes Us Healthy: Helping others leads to experiencing fulfillment and a life of longevity, health, and happiness. Research also shows that compassionate people who have strong emotional bonds and connections with others are healthier, with stronger immune systems, and less likely to become sick than those who do not have positive connections with others. What's more, another study revealed that isolation, or a lack of compassionate connections with others, is as much of a risk to our health as smoking, high blood pressure, obesity, and a lack of exercise.

Giving Compassion Makes Us Productive and Pulls Us Out of Our Funk: Research shows that depression and anxiety are linked to a focus on oneself. When we do things for others, the self-focus dissolves, and we're instantly uplifted, feeling much better about life.[*]

---

[*] Dr. Emma Seppala, "10 (Science-Based) Reasons Why Compassion Is Hot," The Center for Compassion and Altruism Research and Education, Stanford

Arlene said to everyone, "Throughout the rest of Day One, we'll talk about four ways we set out to *Give Compassion* to others—our coworkers, our own leaders, especially our guests, and even our families at home and in the community.

"First, we'll talk about something I'm sure you've heard before, the Golden Rule, and how it will make an impact in our own lives and especially in the lives of people we serve."

University, from the *Huffington Post*, July 18, 2012, https://ccare.stanford.edu/the-huffington-post/10-science-based-reasons-why-compassion-is-hot/.

Chapter 2

Golden Rule

Now it was Nick's turn to lead the discussion. A former teacher, coach, and general manager in his own right, he also had a natural ability to own the room, but his style was inviting as he asked the group, "What does the Golden Rule mean to you?"

Alma, one of the new housekeeping managers, took this one. As she raised her hand, she jumped right into the conversation. "The Golden Rule simply means to treat other people the way you want to be treated. This is a lesson I'm sure we all grew up with, but it's rare to work somewhere that makes this one of the first things they talk about in new hire orientation experiences like this!" She laughed as she finished her sentence. Everyone else agreed with their own chuckles, visibly nodding along with Alma's statement.

Nick put up a quote on the screen.

"Nothing in the Golden Rule says that others will treat us as we have treated them. It only says that we must treat others the way we would want to be treated."
—Rosa Parks, American civil rights activist

"Does this resonate with anyone? How often do we try to follow the 'Golden Rule' only to be let down when others don't reciprocate? Sometimes the hardest thing to do is to keep treating others the way we'd like to be treated, even when we don't receive the same treatment in return. Alma, how do you like to be treated?" Nick invited her to continue sharing.

Alma, a longtime housekeeping manager turned travel agent then back to housekeeping manager in recent years, paused, looking around the room as everyone leaned in to see how she'd answer. "Well, I guess I like to be treated with respect, kindness, care, and really I just generally like it when people are, well, nice," she answered candidly. "For so many years, working as both a housekeeping manager in resorts and even throughout the many years I spent building my dream career as a travel agent, which I still do part-time today, it's always been the kind people—kind housekeepers I've led, kind clients for whom I book travel, and even kind *travel suppliers* whose products, destinations, and experiences I've spent decades learning more and more about so that I can send my own friends, family, and clients to experience them—who have inspired me the most."

As most of the group nodded in agreement, Nick kept the conversation moving. "Most of us would agree with Alma. We like to be treated with respect, kindness, care, and we like to receive these things from others. Of course, this sounds so simple, but that's the point. Oftentimes, the most impactful gestures really aren't that complicated. When life happens, as competing priorities and agendas make their way into situations, we often lose sight of the positive impact we can have on each other when we simply treat others how we want to be treated."

Nick continued, "We get emails and inquiries almost every single week from guests, industry scholars, and hospitality industry executives wanting to know how we consistently create such a positive environment at Kauwela Resorts across our many properties. It really all starts with the Golden Rule. The same things we learned as youngsters in school, at church, or playing our favorite sports really are the same things we try to uphold today in our culture around here."

Nick put up several bullet points to reinforce just how simple the Kauwela Resorts culture is:

- We purposely set out to make people happy, and we become happier in the process.
- We help people believe in themselves, so they work harder, which inspires us to work harder ourselves.
- We encourage people to try new things, stepping outside their comfort zones because that's where they'll grow.
- We build community. We make new friends, building relationships every chance we get.
- We help people have fun, and we have more fun along the way ourselves.

"Let's do an activity." Nick drew everyone's attention to their Participant Guides, which were placed neatly at their tables. It all felt more like a well-appointed fine dining restaurant than a hotel conference room because of the way every single thing was perfectly in its place.

NICK EXPLAINS THE ACTIVITY
TO GET THEM STARTED

Nick advised, "Consider two people you frequently see and connect with in life. Choose one friend and one family member. Reflect for just a couple of minutes and make some commitments for how you will lean into and live the Golden Rule with each person. Once everyone has their chart in their Participant Guide filled out for this exercise, you'll have a chance to stand and partner up with one of your new teammates to share your commitments to bring the Golden Rule to life."

Golden Rule Activity

Choose two people in your life and practice the Golden Rule with them. Make commitments for how you'll treat them the way you want to be treated in the coming weeks:

My friend—I'll practice the Golden Rule with them by:
1.
2.
3.

My family member—I'll practice the Golden Rule with them by:
1.
2.
3.

Everyone slowly but surely stood and got into pairs. Summer Grace partnered with AJ, and as they shared with each other they both took note of the decibel level in the room. What began as a low, soft roar quickly became louder and louder, as slowly but surely their new colleagues were coming out of their shells, one connection at a time.

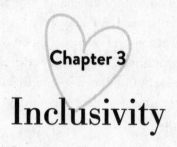

Chapter 3

Inclusivity

As everyone returned from the first break of the day, **Summer Grace** noticed people still gravitating to their comfortable "pods" of sorts. The same people who had congregated together in small groups and huddles prior to the session seemed to find themselves right back with one another at the first opportunity.

While she didn't want to read into it too much, she certainly took note and just sat back down at her seat and waited for Arlene to restart the next conversation of Day One.

ARLENE KICKS OFF THE *INCLUSIVITY* CONVERSATION

With a dose of elegance mixed with her natural state of enthusiasm, Arlene regained everyone's attention and jumped right into the next conversation. She knew this next topic often caused some people to tense up, but Arlene always loved jumping right into *inclusivity* on Day

One because it's an opportunity to help people get comfortable getting uncomfortable early on in their experience together. Those conversations, as difficult as they could be on the surface, seemed to always give way to stronger connections and even more robust conversations among the people in the room as each *Edutainment* experience progressed.

"Okay. Here we go! What does the word *inclusivity* mean to you?" Arlene threw out her usual engaging question to the whole group to get things rolling again.

DONNIE SPEAKS UP

"Are we really going there?" a soft-spoken, yet seemingly seasoned, leader said from the back row. It was Donnie, the new finance manager. "Seems like this word keeps coming up in the media. What's this word have to do with anything we're going to do here at Kauwela Resorts in our new roles? I mean, I'm all about it and all, but is this really what we're doing all week? Just having conversations?"

Everyone in the room could tell that he was clearly exhausted, had been at this corporate America grind for quite some time, and was very clearly "over it" by the way he carried himself.

Arlene smiled graciously and walked toward the table where Donnie was sitting. "Well, I'll answer your second question first. Yes. This is pretty much what we're doing all week. We are having conversations, but not just any conversations at random. We're diving into conversations about the things that matter most. Everything we talk about this week sets the stage and creates a foundation for who we are here at Kauwela Resorts, and the type of culture we've all set out to inspire at our resorts and in all the communities we serve."

"Okay. I guess that makes sense, then. I see where this is headed. So, even though this type of thing isn't my favorite because I'm not much of a talker, we should all get comfortable getting uncomfortable talking about some of these topics with one another, then, huh?" Donnie said with a smile.

"Yes, sir, Donnie! That's the spirit!" Arlene was great at keeping everyone positive as best she could, no matter what. "So, what do you think, Donnie? What does *inclusive* mean to you?"

Donnie leaned back in his chair, looked up toward the ceiling, and dove right into the conversation. "The word *inclusive* means to include others, or another, despite differences in opinion, race, where people are from, or their age. In other words, being inclusive means that we don't dismiss or exclude others from activities, conversations, or any part of our lives for any reason. Although I can think of a few people I'd like to exclude!"

That got a chuckle from everyone in the room, including Arlene and Nick. It lightened the mood.

Summer Grace thought about the "pods" she had noticed forming earlier. She thought this may be an opportunity to get some of her new teammates thinking about the perception of huddling up with the same people all the time. She said, "Being inclusive is to be welcoming and inviting to everyone, regardless of any differences we may see in others on the surface."

"Great points, Donnie and Summer Grace. What are some ways we can *be* inclusive? Tate, what do you think?" Arlene kept the conversation moving, inviting Tate, the new entertainment manager, into the conversation. Tate, having grown up a theater kid passionate about the arts, starring in musicals, working in children's theaters as a producer and stage manager in high school and college, and even having been a supporting actor and performer in multiple musicals on Broadway, was very social, already making friends with most everyone in the group. He was also passionate about this topic. So he jumped right into this one.

"We talked about this a great deal at my last job. Inclusivity is accepting others for who they are, as opposed to who we think they should or could be. Acceptance is so powerful, as we continue to grow personally and professionally. We all have what's known as unconscious biases toward certain groups and subgroups of people who may be different from us. Whether it's race, religion, skin color, gender, or even what side of town we live on or area where we grew up, it's possible to fall victim to prejudging others based on biases we may have." Tate had experienced some less than accepting environments in jobs earlier in his career. Summer Grace perked up, having recently experienced the same type of toxic culture.

Summer Grace added, "Well said, Tate. Being inclusive is the willingness to include everyone in your circles. Whether it's in conversations, sports, activities in or outside of work, or simply how we communicate, being inclusive gives everyone the opportunity to be a part of your world, if only for minutes at a time. This creates a sense of *belonging* for everyone around us."

Summer Grace continued, as everyone else leaned in to hear more from her. "In my last job, when I first arrived, it was great! I felt like I did belong. However, come to find out, it was all an act, from day one. My boss came off interested and accepting in the beginning, but his true colors began to shine through after a while. My boss and other senior leaders there ignored several of us who never seemed to quite fit in. In rare instances when they'd actually engage us in conversations, we could tell they were never really listening to us. It always felt fake. That's why so many of us left. It became demoralizing after so many negative interactions."

Arlene could tell this struck a chord with Summer Grace. "Thank you for sharing that, Summer Grace. We're glad you're here now. And you are right. Listening is the ultimate sign of respect, not to mention a great way to show patience and compassion to others and invite them into your world as someone they can lean on when they may need it. Around here, we see it as not only a great way to Give Compassion, but also a great way to learn more about others, gaining fresh perspectives that may differ from your own."

Arlene added, "So, as you embark on your journey here with Kauwela Resorts, if you ever see or feel someone, or even entire groups of people, being excluded, invite them to join you and your team. They may be shy at first, but you may realize just how much you have in common with people who are different from you. You may be surprised at how impactful that can be for each one of us, individually and collectively as a team. How does being *inclusive* make a positive impact?"

Mary, the new training manager, piped up, as this was a topic near and dear to her heart. She'd spent a couple decades as an educator in public schools in eastern Kentucky, then transitioned to teaching creative writing in high school, and then had been instrumental in creating and delivering leadership development content in corporate America in the five years prior to joining Kauwela Resorts. She was like the kindergarten teacher everyone loved. She had a way about her that just seemed to draw others into her orbit each time she engaged in conversation. She was fun and always had a great time, but everyone sat straight up in their chairs when she took the conversation to a more serious, professional tone. Summer Grace noticed it during Week One and she'd been paying attention to Mary's ability to convey knowledge in the most inspiring and inviting ways without being condescending or demeaning. She was obviously seasoned, but also young at heart with a pep in her step even in her near-retirement age. Arthur purposely brought Mary in to help reimagine Kauwela Resorts' training programs.

She inserted herself into the conversation: "It's great if one or two of us are inclusive, but it's even better when everyone in a group, team, or community is inclusive of one another. When that happens, the next thing you know, you're a part of an entire community of people with strong bonds to one another and thriving relationships. That's when people really feel a sense of belonging. When we're more inclusive, welcoming new ideas and fresh perspectives from people who don't look like we do, grew up in a different part of the world, or perhaps from those who are just different than us, we learn so much more every single day."

Now everyone was leaning in even further as the energy shifted. Nick picked up where Mary had left off, almost as if it were choreographed.

He said, "Mary, that's such a great point. We really do believe in community at Kauwela Resorts. Here's why. This sense of community is also referred to as *relatedness*, feeling emotionally connected to other people or even to a collective cause. For example, think of the great sports teams in history. Their strong ties and relationships with one another made them great. So, we believe in *the Three Cs for Creating Compassionate Teams—Choice, Competence, and Community*. We believe *compassion* is *passion in action*. As leaders, when we give people some *choice* over how their work gets accomplished, we find people really value that autonomy. They're more likely to use their creativity and imagination to come up with new processes, which lead to continuous improvements across the board. We give our teams the development and coaching they need to become *competent* in their line of work, which we've noticed creates more and more confidence. Over time people become courageous and take risks. We also share an ongoing commitment to connection, creating *community* with each other every chance we get.

"The *Three Cs for Creating Compassionate Teams* is our way of creating safe, caring environments for everyone who works here. We've found that when leaders create the right environments, which we'll talk about later in the week, people become self-motivated to give their best effort."

SUMMER GRACE MAKES A NOTE OF THE *"THREE Cs FOR CREATING COMPASSIONATE TEAMS"*

Summer Grace looked around the room and noticed nearly every single person taking notes. *I better write those things down too*, she thought.

Summer Grace wrote them down, the Three Cs of Creating Compassionate Teams—Choice, Competence, and Community. She liked that word, *community*. She filed that away for when she'd get to meet her new team at the front desk. A hopeful feeling of excitement began to come over her, as Arlene regained everyone's attention, taking the group into their final activity before lunch.

Arlene, in her inviting way, said to the group, "Please identify someone in this room whom you do not know very well just yet. I'd like you to purposely choose someone who is different from you in some way. As we all stand and get the blood flowing again, please engage in a meaningful conversation with them and as you learn at least three new things about them that you did not know before, please record those things in the chart in your Participant Guide."

Inclusivity Activity

Identify someone in this room whom you do not know very well just yet. Purposely choose someone who is different from you in some way.

Teammate's name:
Engage in a meaningful conversation to learn three things you have in common with them.

1.
2.
3.

Chapter 4

Validate

After lunch, Nick reengaged the group with another question: "What does it mean to validate and why do you think we need validation?" The question was a little out of left field, as the group was slowly settling back into their seats after lunch.

"Do you mean *validate*, as in to reassure someone that their work or any contribution, for that matter, makes a positive impact? Like, that kind of validate?" Jane, the new sports and activities manager, asked. Jane was an elite athlete in middle school, high school, and college who had turned into a dynamic leader in her professional life. She'd been a cross-country runner and a well-known, well-respected star basketball player in both high school and college. She had an engaging presence, and Arthur tapped into her passion for all things sports, her experience as a leader in high-end fitness clubs, and her recognizable personal brand as a social media influencer when he invited her to join the team.

"Yes! That's what I'm talking about, Jane. Validation. To validate. It can be powerful when we receive validation from our peers and especially our leaders. Why do you think validation is such a key piece of our culture here at Kauwela Resorts?" Nick engaged Jane to go a bit further.

Jane pondered for a second and then listed a few reasons. "Well, I can see how the simple act of validation eliminates our doubts, worries, fears, and even our anxieties. When our coworkers, friends, or especially our leaders *validate* our efforts and contributions, we become more confident. We're more likely to become our best selves, pursuing our own dreams more so than we would have without that *validation*. I hadn't actually thought about it like that, but I guess when I look back at my past roles working for other companies, I never really got very much validation. Actually, come to think of it, my most recent leader where I worked before this never gave me any validation. Maybe that's why I left."

Nick reassured Jane that she'd not only receive validation, early and often, at Kauwela Resorts, but she'd also be encouraged to give it. He said, "When we realize our value, and when others validate our efforts, contributions, and even the thoughts we add in conversations, we're compelled to give that same type of validation to others in our lives, at work and even at home. From the very beginning, Kauwela Resorts has been a place where everyone's value is celebrated. That goes for our guests and our various team members. We'll talk more about values later this week, and you'll have a chance to consider your own personal values, our Kauwela Resorts values, and, most importantly, how you'll bring them to life with your actions."

NICK INVITES ELLEN TO
SHARE HER EXPERTISE

Nick clapped his hands and, with his bounding energy and magnetic presence, asked the group, "So, that leads me to my next question: How can we *validate* each other, reminding one another just how much *value* we have so that we remember the impact we can make when we give of ourselves to others? Ellen, what do you think?"

Nick knew Ellen joined the team with over twenty years of leadership experience working for a global entertainment company with theme parks, world-class resorts, attractions, and even an entire portfolio of full-length animated motion pictures.

Ellen smiled at Nick, as she knew where he was leading her. Arthur had intentionally hired Ellen to head up all recognition programs across the entire brand. So, Ellen took this opportunity to share what they could expect in this new leadership culture they'd soon bring to life. Like Mary, the new training manager, Ellen was getting very close to retirement age. However, her passion for pouring into up-and-coming leaders in the hospitality industry kept her young, and especially young at heart. She wasn't quite ready to hang it up just yet, and she had seemingly found the Fountain of Youth in her many conversations with Arthur about where he saw her fitting into his vision for Kauwela Resorts' aggressive growth plan in the coming years.

"Well, here are some ideas." Ellen stood up as she followed Nick's lead. He'd put a list of ways team members and leaders could validate one another's contributions on the screen.

Ellen projected the list onto the screen for everyone to see as she charismatically walked to the front of the room.

- **Recognize people** with thank-you notes—handwritten, preferably, but also digitally through email, text message, or even social media, showing our appreciation for what they have to offer, who they are, and who they inspire us to become.
- **Follow in their footsteps.** Sometimes, in order to become a great leader, we have to learn how to be attentive followers. If someone you love and respect consistently acts, behaves, or gives certain value to people, you can show them love and compassion by following their example. They will feel validated and compelled to keep being themselves, and you'll feel validation in who you're becoming as well.
- **Share the story.** Few things inspire us and compel us into purposeful action, changing our own behavior, quite as much as authentic stories about ordinary people doing extraordinary things. You and I can validate the actions and special talents of other people by telling their story.

Nick thanked Ellen for being a good sport and so eloquently walking everyone through the list of examples of how we can show one another validation. "Let's give Ellen a round of applause! Many of you know, Ellen joins us with a great deal of experience and she's heading up our recognition programs across all of our resorts. We're lucky to have her here with us for a few months before she goes on a journey implementing new programs across our entire Kauwela Resorts community, at all of our properties worldwide."

"I was about to say, that was amazing! I hope we're all not expected to stand up and give a whole presentation!" Donnie said with a chuckle. Everyone else joined in with their applause, giggling to themselves in solidarity with Donnie.

Nick continued, "Okay, so I stacked the deck with that one. Ellen and I may have planned that little choreography beforehand. But let's keep rolling. When we validate others for their special talents and inspiring actions, how do you think it makes them feel? How do you think you'd feel as the person validating them?"

Jane chimed back in, as this topic seemed to really hit home with her. "Not only does it make the other person feel validated and more confident, but you'll also become filled up with compassion, kindness, and goodness in your heart because of how you made the other person feel. I wish more people did that at my last company. I'm so glad it's a total 'thing' here at Kauwela Resorts. It really does make a big impact."

Nick thanked Jane for her vulnerability in sharing a little bit of her past as well as her thoughts on the power and potential of validation among any team, especially with her new team at Kauwela Resorts.

"Let's do an activity to bring these thoughts on *validation* to life." Nick called everyone's attention back to their Participant Guides. "Before we can successfully validate others' strengths, sometimes it helps to validate our own strengths. Take a few minutes to fill out the chart, and then everyone will share with a partner to get some validation."

Validation of Your Strengths Activity

List three of your top strengths—things you do better than most people.
List how each strength will help you achieve your goals, dreams, and aspirations in life.

My top three strengths	This will help me achieve my goals because:
1.	
2.	
3.	

Chapter 5

Engage

Arlene welcomed everyone back after the final break of the day with one of her simple, yet thought-provoking questions: "What does *engagement* mean to you, and why is it important?"

This time, Julie spoke up. She had recently joined the team as the new beverage manager, in charge of all the bars, lounges, and drink menus at the restaurants. She said, "Being engaged means being involved in activity with others, to be interested in others, or, you know, being committed to others. Is that right?" Julie looked around for some validation from her peers.

"That sounds like the *engagement* we'd like to explore. Very good. Thank you, Julie. What are some ways you engage with each other? Your teams? Or even your loved ones at home?" Arlene, staying true to her style, was practicing what she was preaching as she further engaged the room. "Julie, say more. What do you think? How can we *engage* with each other, inside and outside of work?"

Julie quickly rattled off a few examples. "Oh, sure. Well, we can have conversations with one another like we're doing now, we can play or watch sports with one another, participate in hobbies or activities with one another, and I think the best teams are made up of people who want to learn with and from one another. For example, those of us who've grown up, so to speak, in the beverage and club/bar culture in our professional lives are used to this dynamic. I've worked at many different bars, clubs, lounges, and restaurants over the years, and you'd be surprised which ones were my favorite. As amazing as the five-diamond resorts I've had the opportunity to experience as a mixologist were to our guests, some of them were the absolute worst places to work. On the other hand, some of the most modest-looking bars and lounges many of my closest friends have worked together to bring to life with their creativity and passion for craft cocktails were the absolute best places to work. The difference that mattered most was how engaged our leaders and owners were with us, and how dedicated they were to making sure we had opportunities to engage with each other—at work and outside of work."

"Very nice," Arlene encouraged. "And what is so powerful about simply engaging deeper, on a personal level, with each other?"

Summer Grace liked where this was headed and joined the conversation. "Engagement on a human level leads to a sense of togetherness and community. When we build strong relationships, friendships, and partnerships with one another by engaging in meaningful conversations, we experience life differently than if we try to do life on our own," she shared passionately.

"How so?" Arlene engaged even more, encouraging Summer Grace to peel the onion even further.

"Well, we learn from other people, which broadens our perspective and opens our minds to what else may be possible. With more engagement, more new ideas surface. We also learn to respect and appreciate others for who they are as opposed to judging what we see on the outside. That's what ultimately drove a wedge further and further between my former boss and me. We simply didn't engage with one another. People used to tell me how 'different' I was from the other leaders there, but I always thought we were more alike than we were different. We just never engaged with each other long enough to find out how much we had in common." Summer Grace could feel herself almost reconciling in front of her new colleagues the *why* behind the disconnects she experienced with her former boss in her previous job.

Arlene asked the group, "What do we all have in common with one another, despite differences in our backgrounds, race, color, religions, and where we live or where we're from?"

After a long pause, Jud chimed in. "We're all human beings. Despite many differences, this one, simple area of common ground is consistent among every single one of us—we're all human beings." Jud was joining the team after spending several years as a high school teacher and community college professor. Like many others in the group, he'd grown tired of the politics and toxicity in his previous jobs in academia. So, he pursued a career switch, joining Kauwela Resorts in their learning and development division. He was from Texas originally, so he had a bit of a southern drawl. He was as smart as he was funny, and a well-educated, well-traveled author and speaker in his own right who had joined Kauwela Resorts to settle down with his wife and newborn twins. Arthur saw him speak at a conference two years prior and had been recruiting him to join the team ever since. Jud's energy, passion, and apparent zest for life were contagious, and Arthur knew he'd be just the talent Kauwela Resorts would need to ensure joy and inspiration in the hearts and minds of leaders and teams as they'd grow the brand exponentially in the years to come.

He continued, "Science tells us that all of us—all human beings—are hardwired for social connection with one another. Human interactions and social connections aren't just good ideas for more diversity in thought, more creative ideas, and great ways to learn new things, but as it turns out, connection—a sense of community with one another—is a human need. We all need connection and engagement with one another to stay motivated in our lives and in our work, as well as for our mental and even physical health. So, this is why engaging with other people—our friends, family, coworkers, leaders, and even our guests—will not only help us give the best of ourselves to others, but it will also help us, as leaders, see and bring out the best in everyone we lead."

Arlene and Nick were now standing in the middle of the room as Jud gracefully delivered what could have been part of a keynote speech to thousands! Summer Grace looked around as Jud finished his thoughts and couldn't help but notice some tears in the eyes of not one, or even a few, but in many of her new coworkers' eyes.

"Sorry, everyone," Jud apologized and continued. "I get passionate about some of these things, and I, well, I'm just so excited to work here, with so many other like-minded people. It's only Day One of this week of conversations, and I can already see that many of us share similar beliefs and passions. I'm not sure we would have or could have realized our commonalities if not for these vulnerable conversations with each other so early in the process. These conversations really are so very powerful."

Nick asked the group, "What do y'all think? Do you agree with Jud?"

Everyone gave Jud a standing ovation! Applause from around the room gave way to high fives, which even gave way to several hugs and embraces among those forming relationships early in Week Two.

Nick regained everyone's attention. "Let's do an activity to close out Day One."

Engagement Activity

List one new teammate with whom you'll commit to engaging on a more personal level.

One thing I'dlike to know about them: _____

One thing I'd like to learn from them: _____

I'll engage with them by this date: _____

As Nick and Arlene facilitated an engaging debrief in which several people shared what they'd written down, the following was projected on the screen:

A – *Akahai*

L – *Lokahi* – meaning "unity" (unbroken), to be expressed with harmony and **Compassion**.

O – *'Olu'olu*

H – *Ha'aha'a*

A – *Ahonui*

Arlene and Nick noticed everyone glancing up at the screen and taking in the first line of context added to the ALOHA acronym. Nick smiled at Arlene, and with a side-eye, she winked right back at Nick as if to say, *We're off to a great start with everyone leaning in, slowly but surely getting comfortable being uncomfortable in their new surroundings with new colleagues.* They purposely did not make a big deal about the ALOHA acronym on the screen, as they knew there would be a special moment later in the week to unpack it further.

Summer Grace and several of her new coworkers walked to the lobby bar together to decompress after what had been a great day of simple, yet extraordinary, conversations about seemingly ordinary things such as the *Golden Rule, Inclusivity, Validation,* and *Engagement.* Summer Grace and her new fellow front desk manager, AJ, had already formed a special connection as they'd partnered together in many of the powerful conversations all day long.

They were excited to see Pua for a well-deserved beverage to cap off Day One and prepare for Day Two. Summer Grace bought the first round, and AJ returned the favor for the second round. The two of them had emerged as the ringleaders of storytelling while Tate had already become the "Social Chair" of the group, as he had compiled a list of everyone's phone numbers, email addresses, and social media profiles in a shared file, which he sent to everyone before happy hour was over. Connections were happening.

DAY TWO

Chapter 6

GIVE Encouragement

Arlene wasted no time welcoming everyone back for Day Two of Kau-
wela Resorts' Hospitality Conversations experience. To open up the
day's conversation, she asked the group, "When you think of the word
encouragement, what comes to mind? What does *encouragement* mean
to you? Who wants to kick us off this morning?

LEE KICKS OFF DAY TWO'S CONVERSATIONS

Lee, who will be leading the guest services team, got things going. He
spent the first five years of his career working in theme parks, the next
several years working in some of the most sought-after beach resorts in
the Hawaiian Islands, and for the past few years he'd worked his way
up from being a customer service representative for the largest airline
in the history of aviation to becoming a senior manager of customer
service at one of the airline's busiest hubs. He was excited to be back in
a hotel setting at Kauwela Resorts.

He said, "Giving someone help, support, confidence, or even hope that they can do great things, that everything will work out for the best, and that you're there to cheer them on in any way you can."

"Okay, thank you, Lee. Sounds like you're passionate about this topic. Has anyone ever *encouraged* you, at a time when you needed it? Who was it? How did that make you feel?"

"Sure," Lee continued. "I've had some really great leaders over the years when I worked in theme parks, resorts, and most recently with one of the fastest-growing airlines in the history of aviation. However, something has always stuck with me since my childhood days that I'd like to share. I was always on the academic team in elementary and middle school. I guess I was always pretty smart in every single subject, so everyone expected me to just magically be the saving grace at every meet. But I would often get so nervous with all that pressure. There were so many times when I wanted to give up, but I had a teacher and academic team coach who wouldn't let me. She always reminded me of everything I'd accomplished whenever I'd be in my own head about an upcoming event or meet. She had a way of keeping me focused, uplifted, and confident. I've never forgotten that about her, and memories I have from those early childhood moments and conversations still inspire me to this day."

Jud, with his usual scholarly tone and vibe, piped up once again. "The word *encouragement* literally means to give someone *courage*. It means to lift someone up. Encouragement reminds us just how special, unique, and talented we are. So, it's not uncommon at all to hear stories like Lee mentions about the encouragement his coaches gave him all those years ago sticking with him to this day. That's the power of encouraging people."

Summer Grace, once again, recalled how encouraged she felt early on in her experience with her former organization before things took a negative turn. She felt compelled to share and added, "When we remember how much potential we have, we're more likely to have courage and confidence to keep doing our best even in the face of adversity."

Arlene nodded, pressed her lips together, and said, "That's the magic of *encouragement*. What we're hearing from Lee, Jud, and Summer Grace this morning underscores why Giving Encouragement is another one of our fundamental values here at Kauwela Resorts. Not only do others gain courage, confidence, and hope when we encourage them, but *we* also feel uplifted as well as the actual encourager! We'll spend all of Day Two diving into conversations about four ways we can Give Encouragement. Encouragement is truly a gift for the person we're encouraging, and to us, as the encourager."

Nick charismatically brought up the four ways Kauwela Resorts team members and leaders lean into their value of *encouragement* on the screen. The first topic of conversation was around the idea of *giving their natural gifts* to others.

Chapter 7

Gifts

Nick walked by each table, from the back of the room to the front, turned on a dime, and said, "What do you think of when you hear the word *gifts?*"

Rae, one of the new human resources managers, perked right up! She loved gifts and always enjoyed celebrating all the holidays with diverse teams across cultures and varying faiths represented in the companies where she'd worked over the years. Arthur loved that focus on diversity and inclusion. He also loved her experience as she'd not only worked in the hospitality industry as an HR leader in convention centers, arenas, and stadiums, but she'd also worked for several years in HR for an organization that owned and operated pet resorts in Tampa, Florida, which housed pets for families when they'd go on vacation. Rae had grown up loving cats, dogs, reptiles, and, as she called them, "all God's creatures." So, Arthur recruited her to Kauwela Resorts after meeting her at a Society for Human Resources conference in Salt Lake City.

Rae enthusiastically added, "Holiday time, family, friends, opening presents, joy, happiness, and shopping! And also all the gifts we give our four-legged family members—our pets!" Everyone laughed and some even clapped in agreement. "But no, in all seriousness, *gifts* can be anything given willingly to someone, without payment. It's a present to someone else!"

"All right. Very nice, Rae. Thanks for getting us rolling. Let's talk about *gifts* of your own." Nick had a charismatic way of *encouraging* more comments from others while keeping the group on track. He continued with another question: "Do any of you have *gifts* of your own to give to other people? For example, think about those things you do really well. Think about your natural strengths. In fact, I'd like to ask for a volunteer to share with someone in the room what you believe to be their biggest strength."

Summer Grace recalled Amber's comments from Day One and, with a smile across her face, said, "I'll start this one off, if I could, by recognizing Amber. Amber, I loved your thoughts yesterday around the impact of Giving Compassion. I could tell that this isn't your first rodeo leading teams, and I'm looking forward to learning from you. Your strength is clearly being an encourager and a developer of people."

Amber was touched and gave Summer Grace a smile and a wink as she made a heart shape with her hands covering her heart, as if to say, "Thank you" from across the room.

Nick thanked Summer Grace and held up the Participant Guide everyone had at their tables. "Let's do an activity," he said. "Everyone take two minutes and write down what you believe are your top three natural strengths. These are things you do very well, and they almost always come naturally to you. For some, it may be a sport; for others, it may be a particular area of your work in which you're very strong; and for others, it may be a skill like playing music, singing, or dancing."

Without skipping a beat, everyone began writing notes. Nick and Arlene's *Edutainment* facilitation style created a very safe and extremely caring environment. They were always in control, but in a captivating way—never threatening. The new Kauwela Resorts leaders seemed to put their best foot forward at all times, participating fully in each activity and conversation. Summer Grace took note of the vibe and atmosphere in the room, as she once again smiled to herself and wrote down her strengths in her Participant Guide.

Nick gave everyone the two minutes, and regained their attention by saying, "This is about reminding all of you that each of us has strengths and unique talents, which are *gifts* we can give to others to encourage them—lifting them up and, in turn, lifting ourselves up in the process."

In true Arlene fashion, she threw out another question: "*How* can you use these gifts of your own to encourage others?"

KAYLA SHARES HER THOUGHTS ON *GIFTS*

Kayla, who was brought on board as a marketing manager, liked this exercise. She joined the team with several years of marketing experience in South Florida in the commercial real estate space. She then switched careers, pursued her passion for travel, and became a very successful travel advisor and social media influencer, marketing and operating group adventure travel all over the world. She was settling down with a new family and needed a more traditional role back in marketing in her beloved hospitality industry, so she accepted the invitation to join the Kauwela Resorts team. She offered her thoughts to the group by saying, "I see where you're taking us. So, you're basically saying that each of us has gifts of our own, which are our strengths, that we can give"—she also used air quotes—"to others. Right?"

GIVING GIFTS ACTIVITY

Nick smiled and said, "Precisely. It's a simple principle, but one we take pride in here at Kauwela Resorts. For example, take a look at the slide."

He advanced the slide deck forward and everyone looked up to see the following on the screen:

- Give your knowledge.
- Give your skills.
- Give your encouragement.

Arlene took over and said, "Let's do an activity and apply what we've just discussed to real life and your new adventure here at Kauwela Resorts. Write down how you will use each of your top three strengths as a way to *give* people encouragement. For example, if you're naturally gifted at math, writing, or maybe even presentation skills, could you *gift* some of your natural talent and abilities to someone else, to teach them, lift them up, and encourage them to improve their math, writing, or presentation skills?"

Giving Gifts Activity

Leveraging my *Gifts* (Strengths) to Give Encouragement

My three *Natural Gifts*	I'll leverage each *Natural Gift* to lift others as I climb
1.	I'll give my knowledge and skills in this area to:
2.	I'll give my knowledge and skills in this area to:
3.	I'll give my knowledge and skills in this area to:

After everyone shared how they would give their gifts to others in extensive conversations at their tables, Nick wrapped up the morning session with a final thought. "We all have gifts. Sure, some of us are more naturally gifted than others in certain areas. However, we all have things we do really well. We can all leverage those natural abilities as gifts to share with others. That's one of the ways we intentionally Give Encouragement to each other and our guests every single day around here. You'll soon do the same as you embark on this exciting new season in your career."

The group finished writing some final thoughts down in their Participant Guides and enjoyed their midmorning break.

Chapter 8

Impact

Arlene welcomed everyone back from break with a question to kick off the next conversation: "What does the word *impact* mean?"

Enrique was one of the new safety managers. He'd spent most of his career leading safety and security teams in resorts, convention centers, stadiums, and arenas in South Florida. He was also a former high school and collegiate athlete, and he'd served in the armed forces. So *making an impact* hit home for him.

ENRIQUE ADDS HIS THOUGHTS ON MAKING AN IMPACT

He spoke up and said, "To have a strong effect on someone or something. Also, the action of one object forcibly coming into contact with another, like when I used to hit homer after homer as a baseball player!"

"I love that, Enrique," Arlene said. "You sound like my husband and me, always reliving the glory days of our sports careers. I like what you said about the people part—the impact people can have on other people. That includes all of you, and it includes me. So, Enrique, who has made a positive impact on you over the years? What is it about them that has or continues to impact you in a positive way? How do they make you feel?"

"Wow. That's deep," Enrique replied as he pondered for a second before answering. He said, "I'll tell you about Gloria, way back when I was a first-time security officer at my very first hotel job. She was a tough but fair leader. She was also, I guess, *compassionate*, like we talked about yesterday. I remember one time in my first year on the job working with her, I made a big mistake, which put our entire team at risk of losing control of a large convention exiting our exhibit hall. The way she handled the situation in the moment, basically saving my behind, and how she used that situation as an opportunity to teach me some things I needed to learn, really made a positive impact on me. I've passed on so many of the same lessons she taught me, about how to set up processes and organize security teams strategically to minimize the risk to the company."

Arlene said, "Thank you, Enrique. That's the type of impact we're talking about. Hearing everyone's stories yesterday and so far today reminds us how awesome it is when people make us feel great about ourselves, lifted up, confident, and even courageous at times when we may be scared, nervous, frustrated, or, as Enrique just pointed out, when we make a mistake."

Nick, from the middle of the room, where he often liked to pose his questions, asked the group, "Can you think of anybody in your life right now—at home, on your new team, or maybe even someone in this new hire community—who may need some encouragement? Do you think you could be someone who could give them some encouragement and make a positive impact on them?"

Arlene grabbed her Participant Guide, held it up once again, and said, "Let's do an activity. In your Participant Guides, answer the questions in the Impact Activity, and commit to making a positive impact for someone in this room, specifically in the next week to 10 days."

Impact Activity

Commitments for Making a *Positive Impact*

This person has made a positive impact on me: _____

_____

I'll let them know just how much I appreciate the positive impact they've made on me by: _____

_____

I commit to making a positive impact on the following new teammates by giving them encouragement and lifting them up with my words or actions in the next week to 10 days:	
Teammate	**My commitment to positive impact**
1.	
2.	
3.	

Everyone took their time, thought carefully about each prompt in their Participant Guides, and wrote down their commitments. The activity was complete once Arlene and Nick facilitated a beautiful debrief conversation.

Feeling encouraged, everyone enjoyed a nice lunch together in the Gracious Café.

Chapter 9

Vocalize

Nick welcomed everyone back from lunch, and kicked the next conversation off with a question: "What does it mean to *vocalize*?"

ESTEFANIA SHARES STORIES FROM HER AIRLINE CAREER

"It means to speak up and vocally share your ideas with others," said Estefania, who joined Kauwela Resorts as a bell services manager. She'd spent the first decade of her career working in airport operations roles on the ramp (the teams that work diligently to get our checked bags safely to our destination when we fly) for one of the largest and best airlines in the history of aviation before career-switching to work in hotels in bell services. "In bell services, whether out front in valet or inside handling guest luggage, we must be vocal. Being vocal was also extremely important all those years I spent working the ramp for major airlines at some of the largest and busiest airports in the world. And, since I'm not shy, I had to speak up on this topic!"

Laughs from everyone filled the room, perfectly breaking the ice for the afternoon session. Arlene continued, "Estefania, why is being vocal or vocalizing our ideas or thoughts with others important in our journey to become the best we can be?"

"Okay, full disclosure here: Arlene and I planned this one out too," Estefania said with a giggle. "I actually majored in psychology, with a minor in organizational behavior. So, I've spent several years studying the impact of conversations, collaboration, and connection in the workplace. In addition to my work in the hospitality and travel industries, in bell services and on the ramp with airlines, I've also been a part-time lecturer at my local community college. I teach organizational behavior."

While everyone joined in the laughter, they were intrigued by Estefania's experience and knowledge on this topic. They were leaning in, waiting for her to drop some wisdom.

Estefania got into it. "Okay, so here are some thoughts on how important it is for teams at work, or even families at home, for that matter, to be vocal, sharing thoughts with each other, early and often." She then walked everyone through the following slides and unpacked how the simple act of *vocalizing* sparks conversations, collaboration, and connection among everyone involved. Estefania eloquently shared the following:

- **Conversations:** Sharing ideas sparks conversation, and conversation is the beginning of all positive change—for us and for our communities. *Conversations make good company*, whether in the companies for whom we work or the company we keep outside of work. It's often the *conversations* that make or break the experience.
- **Collaboration:** The more we speak up, the more others may be inspired to share ideas with us in return. This leads to collaboration, or simply working with someone else or other people to make things better. *All of us are smarter than any one of us.*
- **Connection:** When we open up and share our own ideas, we find out just how much we might have in common with other people. That's when connection happens. *Connection with others helps us stay healthy in mind, body, and spirit.*

"How about a round of applause for Estefania, everybody!" Nick engaged the group and continued, "*Giving Encouragement*, showing how much we appreciate special people in our lives, will always create a positive atmosphere around us, for all those who work here and play here."

Arlene grabbed her Participant Guide as a prop once again, held it up, and Donnie, with a half-smile, said, "Let me guess. Let's do an activity?"

Laughter filled the room after the steady stream of great conversations and knowledge sharing.

Arlene, laughing along with everyone else, brought them back. "Yes, Donnie! You know the drill by now. Everyone will prepare for an opportunity to *vocalize* and share a new idea you'd like to initiate in the coming weeks as you begin your new role here at Kauwela Resorts.

"Turn to the Vocalize Activity in your Participant Guides."

Vocalize Activity

Vocalize what you will initiate—an idea for a new process, a new way to collaborate, or simply new ideas for sparking meaningful conversations with your new team members.

I plan to *vocalize* the following new idea: _____

_____

I believe this is a good idea because: _____

_____

I'll invite the following people to brainstorm this new idea: _____

_____

The *positive IMPACT* this new idea will make: _____

_____

Everyone conscientiously put their heads and hearts into the activity, writing down answers to each of the prompts. Once everyone completed the activity and engaged in a lively debrief conversation, sharing their ideas, the group was dismissed for their final break of the afternoon.

Chapter 10

Educate

Arlene and Nick were both former teachers in both elementary and high school. So education was not only near and dear to their hearts, but also among the many topics in which they themselves had the most education and training.

Nick kicked off the final discussion of Day Two, setting the stage for the conversation around *educating one another*, yet another way to Give Encouragement to fellow coworkers and guests of Kauwela Resorts.

He said, "Education, as we all know, is the process of facilitating learning, or the acquisition of knowledge, skills, values, beliefs, and habits. The main purpose of education is to prepare individuals to be fully integrated within our society."

Summer Grace looked around and noticed the engagement level among the entire group. The confidence and clarity with which Nick spoke really captured their attention and piqued their interest for where this conversation was headed.

Nick continued, "Education goes beyond the classroom, as it's not only the usual subjects like science, math, and grammar. Education includes learning how to interact with and become integrated into any given culture with other people, wherever we go in life; and in our case, especially how we interact with one another here at Kauwela Resorts."

Arlene stepped into the well-choreographed dialogue with one of her opening questions: "Why is education so important?"

"PROFESSOR JUD" RETURNS TO THE CONVERSATION

Jud, who was of course also passionate about education, given his experience teaching both high school and college, added, "The benefits of education are many. It's like those commercials we used to see growing up that would say, 'The more you know . . .' When we're more educated, whether from actual school—elementary, middle school, high school, college, or even graduate studies—or the school of hard knocks, we're often more marketable with our skills and the knowledge we've gained. We then find ourselves in the position to earn more money, grow personally and professionally, and the communities we live in or near are enriched as well."

Nick visibly loved this sentiment and the passion with which Jud spoke. Arlene encouraged Jud to keep going. "Okay, Jud! A professor is definitely in our midst!" Everyone laughed but joined in on the encouragement for Jud to go deeper as well.

"In all seriousness, Jud, do share more," Arlene encouraged.

"Communities with larger concentrations of college-educated people often tend to have healthier residents, fewer instances of crime, higher income levels, and even more equality among different races, ethnicities, genders, and age brackets," Jud continued. "That's one of the reasons I'm still active with my daughter's high school downtown. We do all we can to make sure as many kids as possible gain access to financial aid and scholarships so they can attend college or trade schools. It really is important, for so many reasons, to so many people."

Arlene took the opportunity to go even deeper, as she introduced the topic of learning styles to the group. She said, "I'd like to introduce you to the VAK learning styles from a model of learning designed by Walter Burke Barbe and later developed by Neil Fleming."

She clicked ahead to advance the presentation and directed everyone's attention to the screen as she displayed the three types of learning styles. "The VAK learning model divides people into three 'learner categories'":

- Visual learners retain knowledge visually, seeing the information.
- Auditory learners retain knowledge by what they hear.
- Kinesthetic learners process information and retain knowledge by actually "doing" through physical activity.

Arlene went on, "People predominantly learn using one style—whether visual, auditory, or kinesthetic. Though every learner often incorporates elements of the other two styles, they are likely to learn the most through their primary style."

"How can this awareness help you Give Encouragement?" Nick asked the group, as he leaned into cofacilitating this conversation around the three styles.

DAVION FINALLY SPEAKS UP

Davion, who joined Kauwela Resorts as an accounting manager, spoke up and offered his thoughts. "Being aware of the three types of learning styles—visual, auditory, and kinesthetic—will not only help you become more patient with yourself but also other people.

"For example, if you know your dominant style of learning, when you encounter new things, you'll become less frustrated early on in the process. You'll be able to shift gears and key into whichever mode is your dominant learning style, in order to ask the right questions and get the clarification necessary to learn and internalize the new material or skills.

"This helped me when I transitioned from an operating role into finance and accounting roles, working for a few different cruise lines in their corporate offices in Fort Lauderdale, Florida. I learned that I'm very visual, and when my leaders learned that about me, they adapted their teaching and training styles. I learned much quicker, and to this day, I'm able to teach and train other up-and-comers more efficiently because I find out as early as possible whether they're predominately visually, auditorily, or kinesthetically inclined."

"Did y'all stack the deck again? That was some serious knowledge-dropping there by Davion!" Summer Grace said, calling them out on what was obviously another planned teaching segment.

Arlene and Nick both laughed. Davion winked at Summer Grace and said, "Maybe. These two may have asked me ahead of time to share that knowledge with the group. Arthur brought me in specifically to help reimagine the accounting and finance onboarding and training. So, here I am."

Summer Grace, sitting at Davion's table, smiled right back. With an appreciative high five, she gave him props. "Well, thank you for sharing; and for being honest! I'm also a visual learner. So, I look forward to you and your team teaching me some accounting wizardry."

Arlene picked it up there and added, "Remember that everyone has a dominant learning style. You do too. Be patient with yourself and others as you seek to understand how they best internalize and learn new things. Let's do an activity. Turn to the Educate Activity in your Participant Guide."

Educate Activity

Educating Others. Leading by Example.

One piece of advice I'll share with my team: _____

_____

I'll model this behavior by: _____

_____

With smiles all around, everyone dove into the activity. Afterward, the group finished the day with more meaningful conversations in groups, and as one, big, happy family, about each other's dominant learning styles.

Summer Grace looked up at the screen to find another line in ALOHA filled in.

As the entire group migrated once again to the lobby bar to see Pua for sunset cocktails, Amber tapped Summer Grace on the shoulder and pulled her aside.

"Thank you for your very kind words earlier this morning. That was so very sweet, and I was touched," Amber graciously shared as she gently shook and held Summer Grace's hand.

Summer Grace replied, "Well, thank you for your wise words of encouragement all week last week and so far this week. I had a really tough time in my last job with some really toxic leaders who just weren't very kind or encouraging at all. So, I wanted to ask you if you'd be open

A – *Akahai*

L – *Lokahi* – meaning "unity" (unbroken), to be
   expressed with harmony and **Compassion**.

O – *'Olu'olu* – meaning "agreeable" (gentle), to
   be expressed with *friendly* **Encouragement**.

H – *Ha'aha'a*

A – *Ahonui*

to mentoring me as we settle into this new adventure together. I want to learn how to be like you one day. I've been looking for a leader and a mentor I can trust, and being around you I realize just how far I still have to go and how much I still need to learn."

Amber smiled and said, "Of course. I'd be honored to have that level of relationship with you. Oh, and don't worry one bit about what you think you don't know. You'd be surprised just how much many of us have noticed what you *do know*, at such a young age. Much of this just takes time, repetition after repetition, trying different ways of working, messing up, making mistakes, and simply trying more and more ways of working. I have some years on you, so the things you're talking about learning and being able to do, they will all come with time; as long as you keep a growth mindset. You've clearly shown you have that."

The two embraced in the warmest of hugs, and as Amber gave Summer Grace one final pat on the back she asked her, "Would you mind asking Pua if she can make me one of her famous gin and tonics with that hibiscus tonic? I'm going to take my stuff to my room and then I'll be right down to the lobby bar to meet you."

"You got it!" Summer Grace couldn't believe it. She'd finally found a positive, encouraging senior leader whom she could call a mentor. And she ordered herself one of Pua's hibiscus gin and tonics along with Amber's to wind down as the sun set behind the palm trees swaying beside the ocean.

DAY THREE

Chapter 11

GIVE Kindness

Nick opened Day Three by asking, "What does *kindness* mean to you?"

JEFF FROM THE LEGAL TEAM LEADS OFF THE KINDNESS CONVERSATION

Jeff, who joined the Kauwela Resorts legal team as an attorney, took this one. "Kindness is simply *giving* other people our time, a little bit of our talent, or even giving our heart to people. When we're kind to people, it shows them how much we care about them."

Summer Grace sat in wonder yet again, this time at Jeff's ability to at once command the room while also speaking gracefully with kindness flowing from his heart.

Jeff was on a roll, and continued, "This is how I became interested in the law and the reason I ultimately pursued law school and a career as an attorney. Growing up where I grew up, I saw how some people were treated unfairly because of their race, where they lived, or how much money they had. When I was a kid, an attorney who lived near my family would always share stories of how she helped people, mostly marginalized people, seek and ultimately realize justice and fairness for their families. I always loved that. So that's why I wanted to become a lawyer, to help people. Now, I'm here at Kauwela Resorts as a corporate attorney because of this organization's commitment to kindness. I've heard the stories, I've read the stories, and I've even experienced the genuine kindness myself here at Kauwela Resorts. So I wanted to be a part of it."

Jeff had spent over 40 years practicing all types of law—criminal defense, divorce, real estate, corporate litigation—you name it, he'd dabbled in it. He was an older Southern guy who was wise in the ways of the law, but also never took himself too seriously. Very young at heart, he loved a nice cocktail, live sporting events, and was the king of taking long weekend trips to escape the doldrums that often came with being an attorney.

While "lawyering," as he often referred to it, had afforded him a great life, raising two kids with his wife, making a great living over the past several decades, it had become stressful. He'd always been passionate about taking his family on vacation after vacation to the nicest resorts, aboard the best cruise ships, and sitting up front in first class on as many flights as possible. So when he met Arthur over a cup of coffee in the lobby while staying at a Kauwela Resorts property in Southern California several years prior, the two hit it off. Arthur kept in touch with Jeff over the years, and the two formed a bond over their mutual love of sports, resorts, and the very spirit of generosity that made Kauwela Resorts so special. When Jeff sold his law practice, he was finally able to join the Kauwela Resorts legal team, just like he and Arthur had always talked about making a reality one day.

"Well, we're certainly glad you're here," Nick said. He continued with a question for the group: "Why is Giving Kindness important in life but particularly for people like us, working at a place like this?"

JESS JOINS THE CONVERSATION

Jess, the new activities director for Kauwela Resorts, was particularly passionate about this topic. She'd spent the first several years of her career in early childhood education first as a teacher and then as an elementary school principal, but then had spent the past 10 years leading hospitality operations in arenas, stadiums, and convention centers in the same organization as Rae. She'd also worked with inner-city youth in Harlem and in other parts of Manhattan. Kindness was always core to her beliefs and central to everything she taught children and teachers alike in her past roles in education.

She piped up, "When we treat people with kindness, simply being nice to each other, everyone wins. When we're nice to one another, we build strong relationships. Not to be too mushy here, but with stronger relationships, all of us experience more joy and happiness."

"Exactly," Nick said, as he clapped his hands. He continued, "Who doesn't want to be happy? When we're happier, we experience less stress, frustration, and disappointment, and that keeps our brains healthy and our bodies healthy. It also keeps the positive spirit within us alive, which allows us to spread that positivity to our friends, family, and especially our coworkers here at Kauwela Resorts."

Jess smiled, nodded in agreement, and added, "Since we're healthier and much more positive when we experience genuine kindness, our brains function at a higher level. That means, as children, we do better on our schoolwork, and now, as adults, just taller children, when we experience genuine kindness, we perform better in our jobs!"

Arlene laughed, along with everyone else, at Jess's playful yet profound comments, and added a final thought before moving on. "Finally, kindness is proven to be contagious, which means it spreads! When we Give Kindness to others, they become inspired to Give Kindness to people in their lives, at work and at home. And we believe it all starts with us!"

Nick kept this wave of positivity going as Day Three got underway. "We can be the ones who start everyone off on a positive, happy note each day by being kind. As we said on Day One, and as many of you had already noticed, to truly 'give' anything is to put other people first, ahead of ourselves. Giving is all about the other person or other people we are helping, encouraging, or serving with our words or actions."

ARLENE OUTLINES THE ROAD MAP FOR DAY THREE'S CONVERSATIONS ABOUT GIVING KINDNESS

Arlene joined Nick at the front of the room, and set up the day. "Today we'll talk about what it means to be *genuine,* how we can become a positive *influence*, what it means to be *vulnerable* and how that helps us Give Kindness, and finally we'll talk about how to make a positive impact on our *environment*, no matter where we are: at work, at home, and even in our communities."

Chapter 12

Genuineness

Nick posed a question: "What does it mean to be genuine?"

Andy, the new sales manager, took this one. He'd been a successful salesperson in the hospitality, travel, and tourism space for years. Born and raised in Allentown, Pennsylvania, and having earned not one but two degrees at the University of Pittsburgh, Andy was wicked smart and had achieved much success in his life and career. However, he never lost his blue-collar work ethic. That was something his clients and coworkers had grown to love about him over the years. He was passionate about being authentic, both in his personal life and especially as a salesperson in his professional life. He said, "To be *genuine* means to be true to yourself—who you are, on the inside and out. Genuine people are said to be 'real,' as opposed to being fake."

Nick encouraged him to peel the onion another layer, and asked, "Why is it important to be *genuine*?"

Andy responded, while looking around the room at his peers and new coworkers with a grin, "Some people say, 'Fake it until you make it.' Being *fake* is to try to be someone or something other than your natural self. The problem with 'faking it until we make it' is that when we make it, *WE'LL BE A FAKE*!"

Everyone laughed, once again, in agreement and solidarity with one another.

Arlene was now getting back into *Edutainment* mode. She continued with her usual coaching questions: "Who would like to share an example of someone in your life who shows people *genuine kindness*? This is someone who is kind—nice, respectful, and genuine. Share with us what makes them so genuine and kind, how they make you feel, and what their genuine kindness inspires you to do."

LAUREN SHARES HER STORY ABOUT GENUINENESS

Lauren, the new recreation manager who would lead lifeguards and all things aquatic, as well as recreational programming, shared a quick story about a leader she had earlier in her career. "I was in my first leadership role at a resort in Las Vegas, and a vice president made such a positive impact on me, it's stuck with me over the years. I was a part of a grand opening team of a mega-resort, and this particular vice president was special. She was seemingly everywhere."

Summer Grace perked up, noticing that Lauren was talking about a *female vice president*, which Summer Grace aspired to become one day. She asked Lauren, "What did she do that was so inspiring?"

Lauren continued, "She would not only spend quality time with her own team, but she'd also arrive early, stay late, and even work on her days off with other teams throughout the resort. She was of course an advocate for work-life balance, but she knew that the pre-opening phase, while a stressful time, would only be a season. She always reminded us of why we were chosen to be on that prestigious opening team, which kept us encouraged to keep going. She gave her own time quite frequently, putting her own needs on the back burner, while pouring into us, the up-and-comers on the team. To this day, I always look back and recall that we never heard her say, 'That's not my job.' Her kindness, not only with her words, but most importantly, her actions, inspired us then, and she continues to inspire me to this day. We've kept in touch all these years, and she's actually the reason I wanted to continue my career as a leader in the hospitality industry. I was a lifeguard back then. But for the past several years, I've been a leader in recreation and aquatic programs for resorts all over the country. Now, I'm proud and excited to be here at Kauwela Resorts."

Summer Grace took some notes and a deep breath. She thanked Lauren for sharing and knew right then that maybe it could be possible to grow into the senior leadership ranks, after all. *Kauwela Resorts is different*, she thought. It was becoming evident that these safe, caring environments Kauwela Resorts' leaders created made the real difference.

Arlene opened the dialogue back up with another question: "How else can we put *genuine kindness* into action? In other words, how can we give genuine kindness to our friends, teammates, or even our family members at home? Amber, what do you think?"

AMBER, WITH ELEGANCE AND CONFIDENCE, SHARES HER THOUGHTS ON GIVING *GENUINE* KINDNESS

It was apparent that Amber had been intentionally sought out and invited to join the team, personally, by Arthur. Summer Grace was already inspired by her vibe the day before, and now felt extra connected to her after their gin and tonic conversations at sunset.

Amber said, "We can always give others a little bit of our *time*. We can give others a little bit of our talent. Or perhaps we could teach them, sharing our knowledge and helping them get better, and we can always give our hearts."

Arlene was now smiling and looking at a room full of smiles in the audience. The group picked up on the planned choreography. Arlene prodded a bit more. "Well said, Amber. Now, I know you're passionate about this topic. So, could you please share what this might look like as leaders here at Kauwela Resorts? If you haven't noticed, Amber is notorious for building amazing workplace culture, which is why she was so heavily recruited to join us."

Amber put both hands on her heart, bowed slightly as she thanked Arlene, and continued, "Giving our hearts to others is to simply show them we care about them, as human beings first and colleagues second. Take a look at the screen." Amber advanced the slides and presented the following bullet points on the screen:

- **Give your time.** Take the focus off of ourselves and focus on others, to help them, encourage them if they're down, or even tell them how much we appreciate them.
- **Give your talents.** Whatever it is we're really good at doing—sports, certain skills, our passions—sharing those talents with others is a way to show them genuine kindness. Remember your natural gifts we talked about earlier? This is the opportunity to *give* those gifts, early and often.
- **Give your heart.** Simply let those you appreciate know just how much you love and care about them as human beings, not just as coworkers or employees.

Arlene thanked Amber for her passionate and eloquent delivery and kept everyone moving. "Let's do an activity and make some commitments about how we'll give *genuine kindness* to others. In your Participant Guides, write down one example for each of the categories listed in the Genuineness Activity."

Genuineness Activity

Giving *Genuine* Kindness

I'll give my time to my team by: _____
_____

I'll give my talent to my team by: _____
_____

I'll give my heart to my team by: _____
_____

Once everyone finished writing down their commitments, Arlene led a deeper debrief as several of the attendants passionately shared what they'd written down. The feeling in the room was certainly heartfelt by everyone involved. The more one person shared a little piece of their story, the more others wanted to share a piece of theirs.

Arlene wrapped up the morning session by saying, "You've all made some great commitments for how you'll give genuine kindness to people in your lives, at work and at home. I look forward to seeing you give each other kindness in as many *genuine* ways as possible, and especially look forward to seeing how happy, healthy, and positive each of your lives become as more and more kindness is shared."

Everyone enjoyed a nice midmorning break before diving into the next conversation.

Chapter 13

Influence

Nick welcomed everyone back from their first midmorning break of Day Three and opened things up with another question: "What does influence mean?"

Donnie, who had been quiet most of Day Two, chimed in half-heartedly, "Influence is our ability to have an effect on someone, something, or a specific situation. I guess . . ."

Nick thanked Donnie for starting the conversation. "Great, Donnie. And who *influences* you, in your life?"

Donnie said, "My pain in the neck kids!"

Everyone laughed audibly, breaking the ice after the midmorning break.

He continued, "Well, I guess it would be my closest friends, family members, people I work with, and whatever I watch on television. Is that what you're looking for here?"

"Sure," Nick confirmed, and then kept it moving by showing a few slides on the screen. "Here are several *influences* on your life":

- Television
- Sports and Sports Stars
- Family
- Friends
- Coworkers
- Leaders
- Churches or Community Organizations

"So, the question is, why do all these things influence us?" Nick posed to the group.

After a long pause, Arlene met Nick in the front of the room. She unpacked a bit more before engaging everyone else. She said, "It's because of how they make us feel. Science tells us that, as human beings, we're wired to *feel* before we *think*; and it's the *feelings that have the effect on us*. That's influence. It's often those *feelings* that inspire us to think a certain way, do certain things, or change certain behaviors."

As they'd grown accustomed to the cadence of engagement right away when coming back from a break or from lunch, the group was visibly leaning in again.

Arlene continued.

"How do you feel when you watch your favorite television show or your favorite sport?"

Jane, the new sports and activities manager, was all about sports! So, she took this one. "We feel good! When our team wins, we feel great. At least that's how I feel when I'm watching a WNBA game, or when my beloved Kentucky Wildcats basketball team wins yet another National Championship!"

Nick giggled but agreed with Jane; at least, he agreed with all of it except the Kentucky Wildcats basketball part. He asked, "On the other hand, think about what types of things make you feel sad, mad, frustrated, or bummed out. Here's another question: Is *influence* always positive?"

Arlene let everyone ponder the question for a second, and then stated the obvious: "No. Influence can be either positive or negative, of course. What type of an influence do you want to have on other people? Positive or negative?" It was a bit of a leading question, but everyone played along.

"Positive!" Jane said with a double clap and a smile, as her former basketball player roots started to shine through. Her coworkers winked and gave her a nod of agreement.

"Great. Now, let's make some commitments for how we can become a positive influence on others. Here at Kauwela Resorts we do have a positive culture. It's up to us, and it's now up to all of you, the newest leaders in our organization, to keep everyone feeling more positive than negative." Arlene kept everyone moving along and picked up her Participant Guide as a prop, and everyone knew it was time to make some commitments once again in a moment of self-reflection.

Nick gave the instructions this time. He said, "Make some commitments to yourself for how you will *positively influence* people around you. This is about showing kindness to other people with positivity, encouragement, care, and love. Yes, *love*, the four-letter word rarely used in corporate settings! We not only use it around here, but we also put it into action. So, make some commitments for yourself for how you will be a positive influence on those around you in the coming days, weeks, and months. List four ways you will positively influence your coworkers, leaders, and/or our guests, customers, and clients."

He advanced the slides and asked everyone to look at the Influence Activity in their Participant Guides.

> ### Influence Activity
>
> **List four ways you will positively influence your team.**
> 1.
> 2.
> 3.
> 4.

Once everyone made their commitments in their Participant Guides, Arlene invited a few people to share what they'd written down. Once again, the deeper the conversation, and the more one person shared about their own commitments, the more others wanted to share. Nick and Arlene once again had orchestrated a healthy and wholesome conversation about how each person envisioned themselves *positively influencing* the Kauwela Resorts culture.

Summer Grace noticed a shift in the mood. With each conversation, she thought, this was starting to feel less like a job and more like the *meaningful work* she had in mind when she started her previous job. She hoped this experience would stand the test of time, unlike her last place of employment.

Everyone enjoyed another wonderful lunch together in the Gracious Café.

Chapter 14

Vulnerability

After lunch, Arlene started things off with another one of her questions. "What does *vulnerability* mean? Tate, you're an entertainment person, with some great experience in the theater. Unpack *vulnerability* for us, and get us rolling in our next conversation, if you would, please."

TATE LEADS OFF THE CONVERSATION ABOUT *VULNERABILITY*

Tate smiled and perked right up. After giving it a quick thought and framing up how he'd answer such a loaded question, he said, "Being vulnerable is when we open up to others about what makes us nervous, frustrated, sad, or maybe even what we'd like to improve about ourselves. Vulnerability is being able to accept that *it's okay to not be okay*, like Nick mentioned earlier. It's admitting that you have some things you're working on, and I guess, in short, vulnerability is really just being able to admit *who you really are* to others around you."

"Excellent," Nick said, as he kept the conversation going. "How can being vulnerable help us in becoming a positive influence on other people?"

"It shows your humanness," Ellen said right away.

"Humanness? In leadership? How is that a 'good thing'?" Nick put it right back to Ellen, using air quotes again.

Ellen grinned and went into more detail. "Well, it helps you relate to other people. When we're able to let ourselves be vulnerable and share what gets us down or how we'd like to improve, others around us become more willing to share those very same thoughts and feelings of their own. This level of vulnerability inspires people to respect one another the more they realize just how *human* and *relatable* the other person is, which strengthens relationships and trust along the way."

"Very nice. Thank you, Ellen," Arlene said. She continued, "You're a human being. I'm a human being. All your friends and family members are human beings. Everywhere you go in life, everyone you'll ever meet is a human being. Everyone you see on television, and even our favorite movie stars and sports stars, are human beings."

Donnie, slowly coming out of his shell, actually perked right back up on this topic. He said, "Now that you put it that way, we may be different. We may come from different types of families, upbringings, races, and religions, but one thing we all have in common is *we're all human beings*. That means we all have things we need to improve, and we all have things that make us nervous, worried, sad, frustrated, or mad."

Summer Grace joined the conversation again as well. She added, "But it's okay to not be okay. I like that sentiment. No matter how different we all may be, one thing we all have in common is that we're all human. So, at least we can all start there in terms of finding common ground. We can always fall back on that, and better yet, we can always build upon that anytime we differ from or disagree with someone else."

"Bingo," Arlene said encouragingly. She continued, "How can you show your vulnerability to others—your friends, family, coworkers, and even your own leaders?"

MARY GIVES HER PERSPECTIVE ON SHOWING VULNERABILITY

Mary, the new learning and development manager, was feeling this topic as well. She chimed in, saying, "Sharing your thoughts, emotions, and even where you may need help shows other people that you are okay not being okay. You will inspire and influence them to do the same. Many adults view vulnerability as a weakness, but it can be one of your superpowers when it comes to your ability to connect with and even inspire others as you begin this next chapter, leading a new team."

"Mary, thank you for sharing your wisdom. You're here for a reason as well. I hear we sought you out to reimagine how we design and deliver all learning and development initiatives across the organization. Can you walk us through some ways we can lean into our vulnerability?"

Mary took her spot in the front of the room, where she felt so natural, and gracefully unpacked the next few points while displaying the following thoughts on the screen:

- **Ask for Help—It's Okay:** If you need help in some way, ask for it.
- **Share How You Feel—It's Okay:** Be willing to let others in and share with them how you feel in certain situations. The "F" word is okay at work here—FEELINGS.
- **Share Your Thoughts and Opinions—It's Okay:** Express your own thoughts and feelings, as long as you stay respectful. Conversation makes for good company and builds relationships.
- **Slow Down and Enjoy the Ride—It's Okay:** We only get one life, so what a shame it would be if we spent all our time feeling stressed, nervous, sad, or worried. Learning to slow down, be present, and enjoy the little moments will help you enjoy a happier and healthier life—at work, at home, and in and around your community.

"Let's do an activity," Arlene said as she traded places with Mary. The two gave each other a heartfelt knuckle bump, a wink, and a "former-teacher smile" as they crossed paths. Arlene gave the instructions for the next activity in the Participant Guide. "Make some notes for the following questions and challenge yourself to lean into your vulnerability. When you do, you'll also lean into your ability to Give Kindness with humility and respect to both you and those around you."

She advanced the slides to display the Vulnerability Activity, as everyone dove right into their Participant Guides.

Nick went to the front of the room once everyone finished writing down their thoughts. He said, "While we will not have anyone

Vulnerability Activity

I'm Struggling with this part of my life or career right now:

_____

I'm experiencing the following *feelings* at work:

_____

My plan to slow down and take some pressure off of myself is:

_____

share their notes for this exercise, I encourage you to have some conversations with your closest friends, family members, and perhaps even some of these wonderful people you've met this week about what you wrote down. Over time, it will become easier for you to open up and be honest with yourself and others about what, how, and where you need to improve and where you need help. You might be pleasantly surprised with how this will help you build trust with your new teams."

Arlene concluded the conversation by saying, "The more we're willing and able to share and show our humanness, the more others will open up, lean in, and share their humanness right back. It's in those magical moments when trust is built, which of course allows us to lead and inspire each other to reach new heights together."

Everyone was dismissed for their final break of the day.

Chapter 15

Environment

Nick welcomed everyone back in for the final conversation of Day Three. He opened up with a question: "What does the word *environment* mean?"

Julie took this one. As a beverage manager, she was all about her bartenders, servers, hosts, and hostesses creating fabulous "environments." As passionate as ever, having joined Kauwela Resorts from a successful food and beverage career, she said, "Environment is nothing more than our surroundings; or the conditions in which we live, work, and play. We're big on *environments* in our world. Few things are better than great service, with great beverages, in amazing environments."

Arlene encouraged her to continue. "I like it so far. Say more, Julie. Keep going."

Julie willingly continued, "It's everything from the energy in the air, the vibe we feel, and what we see, hear, smell, and touch."

"Environment includes *the people around us*, at any given time. How can we, in our roles as leaders, create *safe, caring environments* everywhere we go?" Nick asked as he advanced the slide to display the following on the screen.

- Be *kind*.
- Be *respectful*.
- Be *helpful*.
- Be *genuine*.
- Be a *positive influence on others*.
- Be *vulnerable*, and open up to others in conversations.

Arlene regained everyone's attention as she picked up her Participant Guide. Everyone knew what that meant.

Donnie stole her thunder and, with tongue in cheek, said as he playfully rolled his eyes with a sly grin, "Let's do an activity."

Everyone erupted in laughter.

With a great big smile and a belly laugh, Arlene kept them right on task. She said, "Turn to the Safe, Caring Environment activity and list three things you'll commit to doing in the coming days, weeks, and months to Give Kindness, helping to create a safe, caring environment for those around you at work and at home."

After everyone wrote down their thoughts, Nick asked for all 20 people to share just one thing they wrote down for *how they would*

Safe, Caring Environment Activity

**Three ways I'll give kindness to create safe, caring environments
for my team**

1.
2.
3.

commit to creating a positive environment by Giving Kindness. Once
again, Summer Grace looked around the room and noticed even more
of her new friends and coworkers smiling at one another, building more
rapport with each thought shared in these meaningful conversations.

Maybe this time it will be different, she thought. Summer Grace's
intuition was once again hinting that this time she'd landed in a role
with an organization whose values aligned to her own. She was more
excited and grateful than she'd felt all week.

ARLENE STEPS BACK UP TO THE FRONT
OF THE ROOM TO WRAP UP THE DAY

Arlene said, "We've talked about four ways to Give Kindness. Being
genuine, true to ourselves, and the type of person we know we want
to be, will always help you Give Kindness. Setting out to be a *positive
influence* on others will help you Give Kindness to others. Learning
to be *vulnerable* and share your thoughts, opinions, and even what
you'd like to improve about yourself will help you relate to people in a

genuine, kind way. Finally, remember that your energy is so powerful that you can actually make an impact on any *environment*, any time."

Nick chimed in, "We all *impact* our environments. The reality is you have two choices. You can make a positive impact or a negative impact on your environment. That's why Kauwela Resorts continues to be a special place for all who work here and play here. It's an incredibly positive environment. Now you're a part of creating these environments. Welcome to a team that takes pride in creating a happy, healthy, and successful life for every coworker and every guest. Welcome home."

Day Three concluded with roaring applause and even a few misty-eyed people sharing a nice moment together at the end of the day. The conversations didn't stop there, but instead migrated to the lobby bar where nearly everyone congregated after an encouraging day of conversations. Hearts were visibly full, and Pua would soon make sure everyone's glass would be kept full of their favorite beverage as well!

Summer Grace was so full of hope in this moment, and as she walked out of the Aloha Conference Room, she noticed the image on the screen once again.

This time, another *Hawaiian word* and its meaning had been added:

A – *Akahai* – meaning **"Kindness"** (grace), to be expressed with tenderness.

L – *Lokahi* – meaning "unity" (unbroken), to be expressed with harmony and **Compassion**.

O – *'Olu'olu* – meaning "agreeable" (gentle), to be expressed with **Encouragement** and pleasantness.

H – *Ha'aha'a*

A – *Ahonui*

DAY FOUR

Chapter 16

GIVE Hospitality

In a slight twist from the norm of the previous three days, Arthur, rather than Arlene or Nick, kicked off Day Four. In his charismatic way, with a warm smile to the 20 brand-new Kauwela Resorts leaders, he asked, "What does *hospitality* mean to you?"

"Taking care of people," Ellen, the new recognition manager, proudly exclaimed to get the conversation rolling.

"Sure," Arthur affirmed, and kept going with a definition and a little history lesson. "Dictionary.com defines hospitality as 'the friendly reception and treatment of guests or strangers; the quality or disposition of receiving and treating guests and strangers in a warm, friendly, generous way.'"

AJ, having been a true student of hospitality, studying the industry in both his undergraduate and graduate studies, while also working as a leader in several different lines of business from hotel operations to sales and marketing, leaned into this one. He said, "Hospitality is simply making people feel welcome, comfortable, and important."

Arthur agreed with AJ, thanked him for adding to the conversation, and kept going with his history lesson. "Typically, when we think of hospitality, we think of restaurants, hotels, resorts, airlines, convention centers, stadiums, arenas, rental car companies, or even cruise ships. Let's take a look at where the concept of hospitality really started." Arthur advanced the slides and put some pictures up on the screen.

Arthur unpacked the following. "In ancient times, of course, there were no restaurants, nor hotels. So, when people traveled on horseback or on foot late at night, they would often knock on strangers' doors and ask if they could spend the night. People would literally welcome travelers into their homes, offering them food, water, and shelter for the evening."

Even AJ, a longtime student of hospitality, was enlightened. He hadn't ever heard that before. Everyone else looked at each other with smiles on their faces, proud to now carry on the rich traditions of good, old-fashioned hospitality in a modern-day era.

"Seems pretty generous," AJ said, looking around at his peers.

Chapter 17

Generosity

"Ah. Glad you went there, AJ. What does the word *generosity* mean to you?" Arthur asked him to go a bit deeper into the conversation.

"Well, I remember from my childhood, we'd always donate food around Thanksgiving time. And later in life, working for some pretty cool hotel companies, we'd volunteer at local food banks and homeless shelters, serving people in need. Last year, when the hurricane swept the entire southeastern seaboard, a group of us raised money for our coworkers and their families who were impacted. We also volunteered our time helping rebuild homes and parts of local businesses that were decimated. So, that's generosity, to me."

"Very nice," Arthur said. "Okay, Jud, our resident scholar. Drop some knowledge on us. Unpack what *generosity* is and then we'll weave it into how we do what we do here at Kauwela Resorts."

JUD SHARES HIS THOUGHTS
ON *GENEROSITY*

Jud perked right up with a smile and got back into "keynote speaker mode." He said, "Generosity is a virtue of freely *giving* gifts to others or to something other than ourselves. It's giving of gifts, like we talked about the other day. Sometimes it could be tangible gifts. Other times it's intangibles such as giving someone a bit of our time, whether we're listening to them, helping them through something, or even helping them with a project even when we don't have to do so."

"Thank you, Jud. You're always right on point with your delivery, and I love the way you're so animated, talking with those hand motions as you speak. So glad you're here with us!" Everyone laughed and agreed, in solidarity with Arthur's recognition of Jud's dynamic ability to engage the group!

Arthur was beaming with pride and now getting into the zone. He further engaged his new colleagues: "Think of a time when you've been *generous* with your time, money, or your own special gifts. When have you *given* of yourself? Close your eyes, and just reflect on how that felt."

Arlene picked it up from there after a long 45-second pause. "Okay, you can open your eyes. Generosity comes from a place of kindness, which we talked about yesterday. As many of you pointed out, kindness is simply doing something for someone or something, without any expectation of anything in return. Has anyone ever been *generous* to you, giving you something without expectation of anything in return? How did it make you feel?"

SUMMER GRACE SHARES A GENEROSITY STORY ABOUT ARTHUR

Summer Grace mentioned her relationship with Arthur. "Well, I remember when I first emailed Arthur. He was busy opening a brand-new Kauwela Resorts property, but I was in such a bad place mentally at my last company that I had to reach out to him. Though I'd only briefly met him at a conference a couple years prior, he made time for me. Not only did he answer my email, but he passed my resume and credentials along to the talent acquisition team at Kauwela Resorts. And, well, here I am. I always felt he was extremely generous with his time and his influence over who gets placed into the hiring pipeline. I couldn't be more grateful, and I said to myself when that happened, 'That's the type of leader I want to be for other up-and-comers looking for new opportunities to grow personally and professionally.'"

"Thank you, Summer Grace. Beautiful story, and yes, that certainly sounds like Arthur. He is generous, and that's one of the big reasons we became so close with him so quickly. Obviously, our brand, Lead with Hospitality, LLC, is all about inspiring the next generation of students, leaders, and citizens of the world to simply live, work, and love from a place of generosity." Arlene's words began to carry more weight now with the group. Everyone clearly saw and felt the deep, personal, and human connection that had inspired the very culture both Arlene and Nick had been brought in to share and inspire at Kauwela Resorts.

Nick picked it up there, and engaged the group further. "When we're on the receiving end of generosity, we feel a sense of *gratitude*. Research shows gratitude, being thankful, and appreciating what we've been given and what we have—whether it's money, friendships, relationships, or help in some way from someone else—makes us happier, healthier, and creates stronger bonds with people."

Jud, having studied this human behavioral psychology phenomenon for years, couldn't help but add, "Something else research reveals is that *generosity* is contagious. When we see someone else *giving*, or when we're on the receiving end of *generosity*, it's contagious. We feel compelled to get in that same frame of mind and *give* the best of ourselves to others."

Rae, the new human resources manager, was also feeling this generosity vibe. She also couldn't help but share what she'd picked up along the way in her research from books, blogs, and human resources strategy work over the years. She added, "Science and research prove that *being generous ourselves* and *receiving generosity from others* makes a positive impact in all of our lives."

"Is this another planned, choregraphed 'participant takeover'?" Donnie said with a playful, yet curious, disposition. Everyone else caught on. The entire room laughed and clapped in solidarity as they encouraged Rae to keep going.

"Preach, girl. Do your thing," Estefania, the new bell services manager, encouraged.

Rae said, "Okay, you caught on to that quickly. Arthur may or may not have asked me to share some research that is core to what we believe and where we want to continue taking our culture here at Kauwela Resorts. So here goes."

Rae walked everyone through some findings, which further *give* credence to the power of *generosity*.

She advanced the slides and shared the following:[*]

---

[*] Jason Marsh and Jill Suttie, "Five Ways Giving Is Good for You," *Greater Good Magazine*, December 13, 2010, https://greatergood.berkeley.edu/article/item/5_ways_giving_is_good_for_you.

1. **Generosity makes us happier!** *Studies show that donating money to others lifts levels of happiness more so than when we spend money on ourselves.* These good feelings are reflected in our biology. Scholars and researchers have found that when we give to philanthropic organizations or causes, it activates the same parts of our brains that become active in times of genuine human connection, trustworthy relationships, and even moments that tend to give us joy.

2. **Generosity makes us healthier!** *Research also reveals that different forms of generosity—giving our time, talent, money, hearts, or resources—are linked to better health, even among people who are sick or elderly.* A spirit of generosity is proven to make us healthier, causing us to live longer, because generosity reduces stress, which is associated with a variety of health problems.

3. **Giving creates strong bonds and social connections among any group of people.** *Studies show that when we give of ourselves, people are likely to give back, returning the favor.* This is not to point out that "getting back" is a reason to give; instead, it highlights the reality and compounding positive impact a spirit of generosity has on others. Giving promotes a sense of trust between people, and over time these consistent positive social interactions lead to strong and healthy mental and physical health.

4. **Generosity evokes feelings of gratitude.** *Whether you're giving a gift or receiving a gift, research reveals that we experience feelings of gratitude either way.* That gratitude, of course, makes us happier, healthier, and more likely to experience even more emotional connections with others. I've heard it said this way: "When we're grateful, it's impossible to be negative."

5. **When we give, we spark a ripple effect.** *Giving releases oxytocin, a hormone that ignites feelings of kindheartedness, bliss, and strong relationships with others.* Studies have found that a dose of oxytocin will cause people to give more generously and to feel more empathy toward others, with "symptoms" lasting up to two hours. And those people on an "oxytocin high" can potentially jump-start a cycle of contagious acts of generosity among groups and cultures of people.

EVERYONE GIVES RAE A GRATEFUL ROUND OF APPLAUSE FOR SHARING

Mesmerized by Rae's presentation, which was backed up with research, not to mention delivered with passion and purpose, everyone gave her a round of applause. Arthur, Arlene, and Nick looked at each other and then glanced back at Rae with appreciation as the entire room continued to applaud.

Nick brought everyone back, picked up his Participant Guide as a prop, and said, "Let's do an activity. In your Participant Guides, make some commitments for how you will be *generous* in the coming days and weeks as you begin your new role."

Generosity Activity

What is one gift you'll give to someone in your life in the coming month?

The person to receive my gift will be: _____

_____

I chose this person because: _____

_____

The tangible or intangible *gift* I'll give: _____

_____

My generosity will make them *feel*: _____

_____

My act of generosity will make me *feel*: _____

_____

Everyone dove into their Participant Guides and got right to work, while Arthur remained in the room. He couldn't help it and addressed the group one final time before leaving them to it for the remainder of Day Four.

He said, "From what I'm hearing and seeing, and hopefully what you're experiencing just talking about *generosity*, we can see how this changes everyone's mood. The very thought of doing for other people, focusing on them, and giving the best of ourselves to those around us puts everyone in a positive frame of mind and allows us to lean into becoming our best. That's what living and creating a generous culture is all about. It's also who we are and who we want to continue to be at Kauwela Resorts. Our culture will always stem from this idea of *giving* of ourselves to each other, our guests, and our communities."

Everyone gave Arthur a standing ovation, and the group was dismissed for their midmorning break. Seemingly with childlike faith, the decibel level from joyful conversations was getting louder and louder as they migrated to the snacks beautifully arranged in the common area outside the Aloha Conference Room. The oxytocin and contagious generosity Rae spoke of was palpable in the room, as a Jimmy Buffett song serenaded the group to their break.

Chapter 18

Inspiration

Arlene kicked things off for the next session with one of her opening questions. "What does *inspiration* mean to you?"

"It's like a feeling of hopeful, enthusiastic joy we get from a moment, a story, an experience, or a person that sparks our creative imagination around what could or should be." Kayla, the new marketing manager, was full of hope and inspiration for her new adventure at Kauwela Resorts, so she piped up on this topic.

"Okay, very good. Thank you, Kayla, for starting us off. Say more," Nick encouraged.

Kayla kept going. "Inspiration gives us so much hope in certain situations because it's ultimately what compels us into action, to want to do more or create something special. That's why I became so passionate about travel. I realized how powerful it was for me, and that compelled me to connect with and inspire as many people as I could to take their dream vacations to inspiring places all over the world. If it wasn't for my baby at home, I'd probably be hiking in Peru with a group or on a cruise in the Western Caribbean right now!"

"Very good. Well said." Nick kept the conversation moving. He continued, "Think about how your most beloved friends, family members, or former leaders inspired you once upon a time in your lives and careers. They evoked powerful feelings inside you, which stirred you up and ultimately ignited a spark that propelled you into another gear."

Arlene came back up to the front of the room and took the conversation even further. She advanced the slides and on the screen were well-prepared, well-researched bullet points. Once again, she jumped back into *Edutainer* mode and engaged the group in a bit of an inspiration lesson.

She continued, "American psychologist Scott Barry Kaufman's article in *Harvard Business Review* points out notable research by Todd M. Thrash and Andrew J. Elliott that shows us just how magical *inspiration* really is. For any leader, in any industry, on any level, here's why inspiration is so impactful."

Arlene used the slides to explain that research tells us inspired people:

- Are more open to experiencing something new
- Set lofty goals for themselves and work harder to achieve them
- Experience more purpose and meaning in life
- Reported higher levels of:
  - Belief in their own abilities
  - Self-esteem, optimism, and creativity

"Take a look at this quote from the man himself," Arlene went on, "who wrote that *HBR* article: 'Inspiration awakens us to new possibilities by allowing us to transcend our ordinary experiences and limitations.'"

Nick further engaged the group. "How can you grow yourself so you can be an inspiration to others?"

"Well, we can read books, blogs, articles like the one you just pointed out, and in today's world, we can listen to audiobooks and podcasts. We can also consume or watch inspirational keynote speeches, shows, movies, documentaries, or anything, really, from our televisions and laptops and even our phones." Enrique, the new safety manager, loved reading books, listening to podcasts, and especially loved documentaries. So, this was right up his alley.

"Great stuff, Enrique. Thank you. We'd all agree with Enrique's thoughts, wouldn't we?" Nick asked the group. He continued, as he advanced the slides, "Here are a few ways we can consistently think about *growing ourselves*, as leaders, so we always have our heads and hearts in the right place to *grow our teams*." He showed the following on the screen:

- Feed your mind.
- Feed your body.
- Feed your soul.

KAYLA SHARES HER PERSPECTIVE ON INSPIRATION

Nick invited Kayla up to the front of the room for what everyone quickly figured out would be yet another charismatically choreographed knowledge share.

He said with pride, "Kayla, I know you've studied quite a bit on this topic, which is a big reason you were so heavily recruited to lead our marketing efforts. With all you've learned about the *magic* of inspiration, you've certainly cracked the code on how to not only create inspiring environments, but also how to tell inspiring stories in your marketing campaigns, especially with the social media presence you've built around your adventure travel business. I'd love for you to drop some knowledge on us for how we can *fill our own cups* to the brim with joy and inspiration so that we can *pour ourselves into others*."

FEED YOUR MIND

Kayla was happy to oblige. She took "center stage," so to speak, and jumped right into it, sharing her thoughts and advancing the slides on the screen to reflect her talking points. She said, "Here are some ways to be intentional and purposeful about feeding our minds."

She unpacked the bullet points on the screen.

Arlene stepped in and added, "As leaders, when we stop learning, we stop leading. The other reason it's so beneficial to feed our minds is, the more we gain new knowledge, understanding, skills, and mental capacity, the more optimistic our mindset becomes. Leadership is largely a mindset game. Now that I'm saying it out loud, life itself is a mindset game. It goes back to *emotional intelligence*, how our brains function in conjunction with our thoughts and feelings."

- Have a thirst for new knowledge.
- Be hungry to learn all you can about every facet of your business.
- Challenge yourself to learn new skills in and outside of work.
- Give yourself time to relax your mind, free of thoughts and stress.

FEED YOUR BODY

Kayla continued, "Okay, next, we'll unpack how we can take care of ourselves physically and feed our bodies."

She displayed the following slide:

- Exercise
- Strength training and cardio
- Proper posture
- Get outside (It's amazing what a little vitamin D can and will do for us.)
- Rest and recovery (Definitely prioritize rest! It's impossible to *pour* from an *empty cup*.)

FEED YOUR SOUL

"Now, for something near and dear to our hearts here at Kauwela Resorts, *how to feed our souls*," Nick said, teeing up the next point for Kayla. "Take it away, Kayla."

She unpacked the following slide.

- **Read books, blogs, and articles.** If you're ever feeling low or uninspired, read something. Inspiration will jump off the page in the way of a new idea, a touching story, or a compelling proposition for a future you could help create.
- **Listen to podcasts, audiobooks, and music.** If reading isn't your thing, no problem. We're in the golden age of podcasts, audiobooks, and, of course, we all have the capability to stream music anytime, anywhere, from any artist.
- **Find a faith-based or spiritual organization.** It doesn't have to be the same faith as mine, nor do you have to join or believe in the same faith as anyone else in your life. Being a part of a faith-based community gives you hope, inspiration, and joy few other outlets can provide. The faith part is powerful, and the community of like-minded people gives you love and support.
- **Share what you learn, lift as you climb.** Often the best way to pick yourself up and climb out of a frustrating season is to share your thoughts, knowledge, wisdom, and skills with others. We feed our souls when we help others improve. That's the magic of leading with hospitality, which is something we believe in wholeheartedly around here. The more we give today, the more we're compelled to give even more tomorrow.

"Thank you, Kayla! How about a round of applause for Kayla taking us to our very own *inspiration station* of sorts!" Everyone applauded, and Nick kept them moving with the next activity in their Participant Guides. "Let's create a plan to feed your soul. Take five minutes and use your phone to find one book, podcast, and organization (faith- or community-based) that you will read, listen to, or explore in the year to come. Write your findings in your Participant Guide. Then, list three people in your life with whom you'll share what inspires you."

Inspiration Station Activity

Inspiration Station—Feeding My Mind, Body, and Soul
Staying "filled up" so I can "pour into" others
One book I commit to reading: _____
One podcast I commit to subscribing to: _____
One organization (faith or community based) I commit to
exploring: _____
I'll share my learnings and inspirations with the following people:
_____

Once again, the group hopped right into their Participant Guides. They filled out the prompts and got into groups where each person shared the most inspiring new book, podcast, community group, or experience they found. Once the conversations finished up, they were dismissed for a nice lunch at the Gracious Café.

Chapter 19

Volunteer

Arlene kicked things off after lunch, as she had each of the days prior, with a question for the group. "What does it mean to *volunteer*?"

Jess, who had given so much of her time to underserved communities, volunteering her time and talents as a teacher and coach, was particularly passionate about this one. She said, "Being a volunteer means that you are giving of yourself in some way, shape, or form. It's about giving our time, our talent, our own resources, or even our own hearts and souls to someone or something outside of our everyday routines. Most of the time, to volunteer means that you are working side by side with others."

"Yes, indeed. Thank you, Jess," Arlene said. She continued, "This connects you to other human beings as you are working toward a common goal or purpose. When you volunteer, you are making connections."

Andy, who loved to get his inspiration from volunteering, to stay filled up so that he could pour himself into *selling the magic* as a salesperson, also became passionate about this one. He added, "Volunteering is a win-win for all parties involved. Those on the receiving end are grateful for the generosity, and volunteers learn that helping others is just good for the soul."

"Amen to that," Nick affirmed as he made his way back to the front of the room, where he engaged the group further. "Consider the following as ways you can start volunteering, paying your good fortune forward."

He unpacked the following points as he displayed them on the screen:

- Offer to help family members
- Volunteer at school functions
- Coach youth sports
- Prepare and serve meals
- Serve in a community organization

Arlene asked the group, "In what ways does *volunteering* make a positive impact? Jess, you're a former elementary teacher and a former principal, correct?"

Once again, everyone knew where this was headed. Another planted, choreographed knowledge share!

JESS TAKES CENTER STAGE ONCE AGAIN

With a smile, Jess stood proudly as if she were back in the classroom. With everyone smiling right back at her, leaning in to receive what the science says about volunteering, Jess did her thing. She shared what she'd learned in grad school: "When we volunteer our own time, giving of ourselves to specific causes or people in need, we not only make a positive impact on others, but we're also blessed with the following scientifically proven benefits."

In full teacher mode, Jess unpacked the next few slides about the positive impact of volunteering:

- **Make a positive difference that matters to people in need.** Making a positive difference in the lives of others brings out the best in all of us. The very spirit of generosity is magical because the more we give, the more we want to continue to give. Once you experience that feeling, your heart becomes so full, and you're inspired to give more and more as time goes on.
- **Gain confidence.** Whether it's right now or in the future, we may not always live or work in areas where we know everyone. Volunteering in community projects with other like-minded people is a great way to meet and get to know new people in our lives. We need confidence to lean into new opportunities with new people. Volunteering helps us gain confidence in ourselves to experience what else may be possible.
- **Become a part of a community.** While we might think we're motivated by money, a great coach, or people pushing us, science actually reveals that we become self-motivated to work harder, believe deeper, and push ourselves to our maximum potential when we experience those Three Cs we heard about earlier in the week— *Competence, Choice,* and *Community*. Volunteering can certainly fill the void across all three of these, but without fail, when we *give* of ourselves alongside others who also share our same desire to *give* and help others, we connect on a deeper, more human level.

"Thank you, Jess. Now, let's volunteer! After that conversation, who doesn't want to find somewhere to volunteer?!?" Arlene directed everyone's attention back to their Participant Guides for the next activity. She continued, "You'll be placed in groups of four or five. In your groups, you'll research volunteer opportunities you can participate in together."

Volunteer Activity

Volunteering commitments

I'll *volunteer* my time, talent, or resources by: _____

_____

Frequency of my volunteering commitment: _____

_____

The impact of my volunteering will be: _____

_____

ARLENE WRAPS UP THE VOLUNTEERING CONVERSATION

Once everyone finished, Arlene invited each group to share with their peers. The positive, inclusive mood in the room was palpable. Arlene wrapped up the session with a few closing words.

She said, "There are so many benefits of volunteering, which positively impacts people and communities we have the opportunity to serve! When we volunteer with local community organizations, it's amazing how simply making that decision to give our time can calm our nerves and reduce our own stress levels. Every single year around here when our Kauwela Resorts teams volunteer, we notice new friendships and special bonds forming all around our communities. We're passionate about volunteering here at Kauwela Resorts. We encourage everyone to find ways to give their time, talents, or money. If this is of interest to you, you'll have no problem getting involved in the many volunteering efforts at Kauwela Resorts."

Everyone gave a round of applause for one another, and especially for Jess, Arlene, and Nick, for unpacking such a powerful message on volunteering. They enjoyed a nice break before the final session of Day Four.

Chapter 20

Experience

Nick opened things up with a question. "When you think of *experiences*, what comes to mind?"

Summer Grace was passionate about experiences in general. She'd experienced some cool moments, but also some difficult ones in her life and career up to that point. She took this one and said, "To me, an experience is something that you do or something important that affects you. It's living through certain events, observing, and feeling something in the moment."

"Excellent. Thanks for kicking us off, Summer Grace," Nick said with a smile and his patented clap. He engaged further: "What are some different types of experiences that may shape how we think, how we feel, and even what we know?"

Summer Grace kept going. "In life there are several ways we can gain experience, which ultimately gives us knowledge, skills, and understanding we may not have gained otherwise. With every experience, we gain more knowledge, perspective, and confidence."

Arlene then asked, "Why do we gain more confidence when we seek out and lean into different kinds of experiences?"

Jane, who was all about experiences, especially with her sports background, piped up on this topic. She said, "The more we experience in life, the more we get outside our comfort zones. Just like with working out or performing as an athlete, we don't get stronger until we put some stress on our bodies and minds, taxing ourselves mentally and physically. Sure, during a very strenuous workout, it's uncomfortable. However, what happens next time? The next time we perform the same exercise or find ourselves in similar, physically taxing or mentally stressful situations, we're slightly more comfortable with it. That's growth."

Jud picked up on this conversation next. He added, "The same goes for our mental well-being and ability to grow our mental capacity, learning new skills. Consider the first time we study algebra, geometry, or physics. It seems like it's a completely different language. However, with time, through conversations with each other, and education from our teachers, the subject matter becomes less and less 'uncomfortable' as we practice."

Jane was feeling this vibe, and jumped right back into the conversation. "The next thing we know, we understand the basics of algebra, physics, and geometry, or any other subject matter that may have been daunting at first. That's the growth I'm talking about. Good point, Jud."

"I love where this is going," Nick said. "And the same goes for our emotional intelligence and how we're able to think through situations as leaders in professional settings. Emotional intelligence, like we mentioned earlier, is how well we're able to understand our own feelings, thoughts, and emotions as well as feelings of other people so that we respond positively in situations as opposed to reacting negatively."

Donnie, once again on the fence, asked with a bit of a sarcastic tone, "What does this have to do with experiences?"

SUMMER GRACE CONNECTS WITH DONNIE IN A MEANINGFUL WAY

Summer Grace had been listening to Donnie since Day One. While she was annoyed at first, she was now noticing there could be hope for a relationship with him after all!

She took this opportunity to further engage, adding her thoughts. "The more experiences we have that challenge us emotionally and socially to step outside our comfort zones, the sooner we'll grow, progress, and mature from those challenges. Remember this saying—'No challenge, no change'? For example, the first time we experience a disappointing situation—a bad review from a boss, a best friend moves away, losing a client, or an argument with someone we love—it's extremely hard to deal with it. We have a difficult time coping with our feelings and thoughts."

"Yeah. So?" Donnie was leaning in, but still not quite on the same page.

Summer Grace was rolling now. "However, what happens next time? After having been challenged with the prior experience, we still feel the disappointment or sadness in certain situations, but we have more confidence in our ability to pick ourselves up, dust ourselves off, and keep moving ahead, because we're still standing despite the sadness we experienced last time."

Nick added, "We've grown. We've matured. And we believe we can still move on and move forward in our lives to experience even more—the good, the bad, and the ugly."

Donnie now was nodding along. He said, "Okay, so with each experience, we learn more about ourselves and how to interact with other people. Makes sense."

"Yes!" Arlene could feel the room coming back together. She took this "teachable" moment to jump back into *Edutainer* mode and dive deeper into how some moments are more impactful than others. She advanced the slides forward and displayed some enlightening thoughts on how magical experiences impact us.

She said, "There are four ways *moments,* or experiences, in our lives shape who we ultimately become. When these moments happen, we certainly go through an experience right then, but we're often changed on the inside, which helps us cope with similar challenges we may very well face again in the future. We also learn how to appreciate the positive moments—the moments that matter most—along the way."

She unpacked the following points as she displayed them on the screen. Everyone was not only leaning in, they were also taking notes.

Moments That Matter:

1. **G**ive us joy—Elevating our emotions in a positive and enjoyable way. Certain moments like celebrations, holidays, weddings, births of children, or winning games or awards of any kind elevate our sense of joy and happiness. So those are moments in time that matter to us. We realize what brings us joy, so we're more inclined to seek out more of those types of experiences.

2. **I**nspire us—We become inspired, and we become filled with pride. This is the "good pride," when we become either *proud of ourselves* or *proud of someone else* for what they've just accomplished. For example, we're proud when we see a sibling or niece, nephew, son, or daughter do well in school or in sports. We're proud and inspired when we tackle a difficult assignment or project and come out on the other side having produced something great or worthwhile for our teams and organizations. Those moments give us reason to seek out more moments like them because they matter to us and shape who we're becoming.

3. **V**ision—We gain insight into what could be, should be, or even what we can accomplish with clear vision for a future we can create together. In some moments, we learn. This includes the good, bad, and ugly moments. Even when we go through challenging times, experiencing loss, sadness, disappointment, or frustration, we gain insight. We learn from our own mistakes and from mistakes others have made. The important thing is that we learn from those moments so that when faced with a similar experience in the future, we don't make the same mistake twice. As we experience more and more moments, we begin to formulate a clearer picture and vision for what we can do differently or more frequently, as we create the best possible future for ourselves and others.

4. **E**quality—We realize the power of human connection, regardless of differences in race, color, creed, religion, or orientation. As we grow, emotionally and socially, it's through certain moments that we begin to realize, despite all our differences, we have one thing in common, as we've alluded to many times this week—we're all human beings. We were all created equally, and when we treat everyone equally, with respect, kindness, grace, and ALOHA, we experience connection. Science and research reveal that all humans are wired for connection, as many have pointed out in our conversations this week. We need it, we crave it, we desire it, and we thrive in moments of connection with other people.

Donnie was inspired. He was now smiling, and said, "So the more we can experience *connection* with others, through meaningful conversation, despite how different we may be on the outside, the more we'll experience positive emotions of appreciation, gratitude, and respect on the inside? Maybe I should have ventured outside my office, away from my desk where I was neck deep in spreadsheets, more in my last job. Perhaps I wouldn't have been so annoyed with all those humans I had to babysit with their incorrect expense reports."

"You've got it, sir," Arlene encouraged, as she laughed out loud. She continued, "Experiencing these moments—big and small—helps shape our ability to create positive experiences for everyone with whom we interact, wherever we go in life and especially doing what we do here at Kauwela Resorts for each other and for our guests."

ARLENE AND NICK BRING THE *EXPERIENCE* CONVERSATION TO LIFE WITH AN APPLICATION

Arlene took them into their final activity of the day. "Consider an *experience* you've had which resulted in feeling at least one or multiple of the following feelings."

- A moment that **G**ave you joy.
- A moment that **I**nspired you and made you proud.
- A moment that gave you a clearer, or new, **V**ision of how things could be, should be, or would be if only some significant changes occurred.
- A moment that gave you a sense of **E**quality as you realized all the things you had in common with someone else who on the surface looks different than you, or may be different than you.

"Take your time and fill out the table in your Participant Guide. When you've completed this exercise, you'll be reminded of the things that motivated you in the past and will likely motivate and inspire you in the future. These are also the very *moments* we're here to create for our guests and each other in our roles in the show at Kauwela Resorts."

Experience Activity

Experience Reflection
This *EXPERIENCE* **G**ave me joy, **I**nspired me, sparked a new **V**ision, and reminded me about **E**quality.

This *experience* **G**ave me joy because: _____
_____

This *experience* **I**nspired me because: _____
_____

This *experience* gave me a new **V**ision for: _____
_____

This *experience* reminded me of the power of human connection
and **E**quality because: _____
_____

STORIES ABOUT MOMENTS THAT MATTER

For the next 45 minutes, every single person shared a story of an experience that had moved them in some way. Everyone looked around at one another. Summer Grace had a little "moment" of her own as she noticed all the different faces, from so many different places, representing so many different races, and she couldn't help but notice how different this really felt.

For once, she found herself working in a place where several people looked like her. She was also pleasantly surprised with how everyone was learning from and inspiring each other.

They were learning from conversations—old-fashioned, well-intended, meaningful conversations. This didn't happen in her last job.

She was filled with hope in that moment, and she had a feeling she'd continue to feel hope as long as she and her new peers continued to have these types of conversations.

"Thank you for sharing insights you've gained from experiencing moments that matter." Nick had a way about him that always seemed to land each point. He continued, "As you can see, the more we *experience*, whether the moments are good, bad, or even ugly, we learn, grow, and mature. This is what helps us blossom and become the best versions of ourselves while inspiring us to look for and appreciate the very best in others, despite our differences."

Everyone stood up and proudly gave each other a standing ovation.

DONNIE SURPRISES EVERYONE

Donnie, to the surprise of many in the room, jumped back into the dialogue almost as if yet another light bulb had just turned on above his head. "This is crazy. I don't know about everyone else, but as I was sitting here reflecting on a couple moments that really did give me joy, a sense of inspiration, a clear vision for what I wanted in my future, and even that bit about leaning into equality, I'm now even more compelled and inspired to create those same types of moments for people on my team and our guests here at Kauwela Resorts."

Arlene and Nick locked eyes and couldn't help but smile proudly. Nick wrapped up the day with some closing thoughts. In every session they deliver, there are always one or two people who seemingly have their guard up at the beginning but tend to come around by the end of the experience. That was the magic of their *Edutainment* style of facilitating. It was less about the words they'd say or the dazzling content on the screen or in Participant Guides. It was all about the safe, caring environment they were able to magically create through Hospitality Conversations.

"If you haven't noticed, the reason we've been so successful for so many years here at Kauwela Resorts is because of our commitment to connection with one another. We simply commit to engaging each other in conversations about the things that matter, just as each of you have leaned into these conversations all week; and that last one was especially meaningful. Donnie, thank you so much for sharing. I'm sure I speak for everyone when I say that your comments reminded all of us why we're here, with this opportunity to have more than just a job, but instead, truly meaningful work. We'll dive into our approach to leadership tomorrow. Have a great night, everyone."

Tate invited everyone to a show that night in the Lahaina Theater, which featured many of his new entertainment team members. Hearts were full yet again and the decibel level crept right back up as everyone congregated, engaging in conversations about drinks, dinner, and what everyone would wear for their evening together.

Summer Grace smiled from ear to ear on her way out of the Aloha Conference Room as she noticed the same ALOHA image projected on the screen. This time, yet another word with its meaning was added:

A – *Akahai* – meaning "**Kindness**" (grace), to be expressed with tenderness.

L – *Lokahi* – meaning "unity" (unbroken), to be expressed with harmony and **Compassion**.

O – *'Olu'olu* – meaning "agreeable" (gentle), to be expressed with **Encouragement** and pleasantness.

H – *Ha'aha'a* – meaning "humility" (gentle), to be expressed with **Hospitality**.

A – *Ahonui*

DAY FIVE

Chapter 21

GIVE Leadership

Arlene welcomed everyone back for their fifth and final day of conversations, rounding out Week Two with one of her thought-provoking questions.

"How would you define *leadership*?" she asked the group. "Give that some thought as we get warmed up for our conversations around how we approach *leadership* here at Kauwela Resorts."

"Bossing people around!" Donnie said, all of a sudden in a much more lighthearted mood, and playfully getting things rolling to start the day. As everyone giggled, Donnie, with a smile and a wink to Arlene, continued. "I'm kidding, I'm kidding. Earlier in my career I thought that's what leadership was all about. However, I was humbled quickly in my first leadership role several years ago, and to be honest, I'm still learning how to pull it off. But I think leadership comes down to getting results with and through other people's talents. Or something to that effect."

Nick validated Donnie with appreciation for starting things off.

"Well said, Donnie. Anyone else care to share their definition of leadership? Ellen? Jud?"

Ellen and Jud locked eyes, and with her genuine smile and a wink of her own, Ellen gestured as if to invite Jud to take it away.

"How about this definition . . ." Jud stood up as if it were another one of his keynote speeches, and said, "Leadership is all about inspiring and motivating *the right behaviors, at the right time, to further a collective purpose, to achieve agreed-upon results.*"

Donnie sarcastically said, "Well, that's what I meant."

The ice had officially been broken as everyone laughed out loud. Arlene regained everyone's attention, thanked Jud once again for his words of wisdom, and unpacked what she called the Six Virtues of Leading with Hospitality,[*] which would set the stage for the day's conversations on what it meant to be a leader at Kauwela Resorts. She advanced the slides on the screen and walked through the following:

The Six Virtues of Leading with Hospitality

1. **Connect:** *Have a commitment to connection.*
2. **Strive for Self-Mastery:** *Have a growth mindset to always "better your best."*
3. **Serve:** *Think about leadership as selfless service to others.*
4. **Engage:** *Be purposeful in how you engage with others—Guest first, Team always.*
5. **Coach:** *With grace, grit, and intention.*
6. **Inspire:** *Inspire yourself and others.*

---

[*] For more on these virtues, see Taylor Scott, *Lead with Hospitality: Be Human. Emotionally Connect. Serve Selflessly.* (BenBella Books, 2021).

Arlene said, "You'll see us again and again as you get further into your first few months on the job as Kauwela Resorts leaders. We have specific learning experiences you'll be invited to take part in where we'll dive deeper into each of these six virtues. For today, however, we'll focus our conversations around four simple but not always easy ways we live and breathe our fifth Kauwela Resorts core value—*Give Leadership*. The conversations today will be on the following topics: *Gratitude*, *Intentionality*, *Values*, and *Empathy*."

At that moment, Arthur, who had been quietly hanging out in the back of the room, said, "Congratulations. Up until now, you've all been great *doers*. Now, you're leaders. You're Kauwela Resorts leaders, and that takes on a whole new set of responsibilities. Whereas before, your success may have been a function of *how well you performed, and it was all about what you, yourselves, were able to do*, now your success as a leader will be a function of how well you can inspire other people to perform. Leadership to us is all about *how well we're able to take mere groups of people, turn them into high-performing teams of people, and then go lead them to deliver their magic so that we achieve our collective, agreed-upon results together*."

Summer Grace looked down at the goose bumps on her arms as she smiled to herself. *This would definitely be more like it*, she thought. This type of leadership was what she *thought* her job with her last company would entail. A feeling of relief and gratitude came over her as she looked around the room, noticing every single one of her new colleagues diligently taking notes, capturing what Arthur just said.

Chapter 22

Gratitude

Nick picked it up right there and kicked off the leadership conversa-tions, as usual, with a question. "What does *gratitude* mean?"

Davion, one of the new accounting managers, piped up and said, "It's being thankful for what you have or what others do with and for you. Gratitude hits home with me. In the past five years, my career has been so up and down. I've started and lost three jobs in such a short period of time. So, to be here, at a place like this, with a culture like this, and now, after getting to know all of you on such a personal level, *gratitude* is definitely my word of the day, month, and year." His voice cracked ever so slightly, as he looked around the room at his new peers and fellow coworkers.

Arlene said, "Thank you, Davion. I can tell you're incredibly authentic with those sentiments. We're glad you're here. Gratitude rhymes with *attitude*, and as Davion just shared, it means to have a thankful and pleasing feeling about what you've received from someone else. When we feel gratitude, we're *pleased* with what someone else did for us or how they treated us. The magic of letting yourself feel gratitude is that you're simply so thankful and appreciative of someone else that you're not anxious about having to pay anything back to them. However, it is important to show them you're grateful, as I'm sure everyone here knows all too well."

Nick picked it up from there. "What does it mean to be grateful? Lauren, any thoughts?" He looked right at Lauren, the new recreation manager.

"Gratefulness means 'to be full of heart.' Someone actually mentioned this earlier, and it's worth repeating. When we appreciate all we have and all the good in our lives, it's impossible to be negative—sad, mad, nervous, or frustrated."

"Well said, Lauren. Thank you," Nick said as he advanced the slides to display some thoughts on gratitude on the screen. He continued, "Having 'an attitude of gratitude' will help you . . ."

- Experience more positive emotions, which keep you lifted up and encouraged.
- Enjoy your life for what you do have as opposed to dwelling on things you don't have.
- Overcome stressful, worrisome situations.

Arlene picked it up from there, and centered the conversation on Kauwela Resorts' leadership philosophies. "When it comes to leadership, how can we show people on our teams just how grateful we are for them and what they do for our organization?"

GRATITUDE STORIES INSPIRE EVERYONE

Donnie, who had been seemingly on the fence the entire week, but close to a breakthrough the day before, jumped in with his comments on this one. "We can tell them in conversations. Sometimes simply saying the words *thank you* means the most. It's also special when we take the time to write them a thank-you note. Other times, we can show them with our actions." Donnie was visibly distraught, slouching back in his chair.

He looked around the room, paused for a second, and then continued sharing. "This one hits home for me because one of the big reasons I'm here is because I wasn't very well liked in my last job. I was given some feedback on my way out the door, which really impacted me. Though I made the decision to leave the company on my own, if I hadn't left voluntarily, I would have been asked to leave eventually. The writing was on the wall.

"My last general manager told me all of my peers and several of my team members had gone to him with frustrations about the way I never thanked anyone for anything. The feedback was that I was always so wrapped up in my own agenda, my own analysis, my own spreadsheets, conference calls, and my story of what I was contributing to the organization.

"So, as everyone's been sharing stories this week, I've decided that another great way to show our gratitude is to tell stories about our valued peers, leaders, and especially those on our teams, as a meaningful way to recognize them. They'll know how much we appreciate them when we tell stories about them, as opposed to telling stories of our own awesomeness, like I tended to do in my last role."

Arlene walked over to Donnie, extended her hand, and Donnie shook it with a smile. "Donnie, it's been so cool to see you slowly open up a little more each day this week. Something tells me this experience, working here, will be a bit more fulfilling for you and for everyone on your team."

HANDWRITTEN NOTES OF GRATITUDE

Nick grabbed a stack of Kauwela Resorts stationary with a pineapple, palm tree, and a heart engraved atop the company logo, held it up high, and said, "Let's do an activity."

Arlene gave the instructions as she passed out the thank-you note cards. "In your Participant Guides, you'll see a chart with opportunities to write down why you're grateful for up to five people in your life. You'll notice we've listed a mix of personal and professional relationships for you to consider. Please choose one of them, and write a note of gratitude to one person—a friend, family member, one of your new coworkers, a team member, or maybe even your own leader—who has taught you something, helped you with something, or inspired you in some way. Write them a personal, handwritten note and either hand-deliver it to them or send it by mail."

Gratitude Activity

I will write a handwritten note of gratitude to the following people:

People in my life	I'm grateful for each because
A friend	
A family member	
A new coworker	
A team member	
My own leader	

Everyone jumped right into it, writing their notes of gratitude to their chosen recipients. As Summer Grace looked around while finishing up her note to Arthur, she couldn't help but see and hear some of her coworkers sniffling. Some had been moved to tears as they reflected and wrote their notes of gratitude.

"How did it feel to write down how much you appreciated that special person?" Nick asked the group.

ATTITUDES OF GRATITUDE

Nobody raised their hand or spoke up right away. As Summer Grace continued to look around, she noticed just how *moved* everyone was.

She spoke up and said, "This is one of those things that I'm sure we all know we should do far more frequently than we do. The impact on the other person receiving the note is special, but just reflecting on this, from a place of gratitude and actually putting it into words on a card, really did something to me on the inside. I can't help but think everyone else had a similar experience."

Everyone in the group nodded their heads in agreement, some wiping away tears, while smiling through their emotions.

Arlene wrapped up the morning session with a final thought. "When we let ourselves first feel a sense of gratitude, and especially when we show our gratitude for others, we experience the positive emotions that keep us inspired to inspire others. That's why our approach to leadership starts with *greeting people with gratitude* every chance we get.

"Leadership, to us, is all about connecting with and inspiring other people to become their absolute best. In order to do that, we know we, as leaders, must strive to become our best, leading ourselves first, before we can effectively lead others. This all starts with emotional intelligence, which in many ways starts with keeping ourselves in a positive and upbeat mood so that we can inspire the same positivity among our teams who work so hard every single day."

Everyone applauded for Arlene, Nick, and in solidarity with a proverbial "amen" to all they just heard and experienced in their conversation about gratitude. The group was dismissed for their morning break.

Chapter 23

Intentionality

Arlene made her way back to the front of the room following the first midmorning break. "Welcome back from break, everyone. Thank you for being intentional in how you made your way back to us on time." She winked at a few people sitting toward the front of the room and gave the entire group an engaging smile, as she charismatically regained everyone's attention.

"That's what we'll talk about in this next section before we take a break for lunch: *intentionality*. Sometimes even when we have the best of intentions, we fall short, and in doing so, others may not get to see the best of who we are and what we have to offer," she continued as everyone was again leaning in and on the edges of their seats.

"What does it mean to be *intentional* with our actions and why do you think this is so important in creating environments for groups of people to transform into high-performing teams of people?" Arlene posed the question to the group.

"I think about where I worked prior to here, and I have so many instances where my former leaders may have been well-intended in their own minds, but too often we just didn't see their actions quite measure up to what they'd either promised or intended," answered Johnnie, the new facilities manager joining the Kauwela Resorts family. "So, it seems like *being intentional* with our actions is not only thinking or talking about what you're going to do, but also actually doing it. Is that right?" Johnnie was now looking around for some validation.

Johnnie had been a bit of a journeyman, working on engineering and maintenance teams and then as a leader in the technical operations division of not one but two airlines in recent years. His experiences as a frontline technician were rocky, to say the least, when he was younger. He had really bad experiences with very poor, critical, and rude leaders. So, he purposely went to a trade school, became an aircraft maintenance technician, got a job with his favorite airline, and absolutely loved it. He finally had some inspirational leaders who encouraged him to become a lead, then a supervisor, then a manager. He'd come into his own as a leader and an amazing developer of engineering and maintenance teams. So much so that he was featured in his most recent airline employer's magazine a year prior. Arthur, always on the lookout for great talent, was inspired by his story, reached out to him, and recruited Johnnie to join the Kauwela Resorts team as a facilities manager.

INTENTIONALITY: DOING THINGS ON PURPOSE, WITH A PURPOSE, FOR A PURPOSE

"Bingo, Johnnie," Arlene said and then continued, "Being *intentional* is when we do things on purpose, with a purpose, for a purpose. It's when we're aware of what we want to do and then follow through, doing all we can to make it happen. It's about setting a goal and then going for it! Usually, we become intentional with the most important things in our lives—people we love and respect, things we want to accomplish, or becoming who we want to become. The key is to make sure our intent is visible to other people. To Johnnie's point, it's one thing to have intent, but it's something completely different to become someone who's intentional with their actions."

Arlene threw out her next question: "How can we be *intentional* with our actions? Where does this start?"

Summer Grace recalled her own former boss, Derek, at the company she recently left to join Kauwela Resorts. Derek tended to be all talk and no action, but down the stretch, he didn't even block out time to connect with Summer Grace or her teammates.

"It starts on the inside, with our thoughts," Summer Grace contributed to the discussion.

"What do you mean? That's an interesting point, Summer Grace. Say more," Arlene encouraged.

Summer Grace continued, speaking from a place of passion and purpose, having recently gone through what started out as a great work experience but quickly took a negative turn. "When we become more thoughtful about how to make the best use of our time—at work or at home—we become nicer, more trustworthy people because we *think before we speak*, and we *speak with purpose*. We become more productive because everything we do helps us, or others, get closer to what they want in life."

"Ah. So, intentionality starts in our hearts and minds. Is that what you're saying?" Arlene smiled as she further engaged the group in the conversation.

"For sure," Summer Grace added.

"Okay. The question for us, then, is how can we become more intentional with our thoughts? Let's hear from someone we haven't heard from yet. Bill, what do you think?" Arlene was a pro, making sure to invite everyone and anyone into the conversation, making it a safe environment for learning and collaboration.

"We can choose positivity over negativity. The best way to stay positive—happy, in a good mood, and enjoying life—is to focus on what you are grateful for. Focusing on what you *have* instead of dwelling on what you *don't have* will always keep you in an upbeat and positive mood. It's impossible to be negative when we're grateful, just like someone was saying yesterday." Bill answered with some intentionality of his own, piping up from the back of the room where he was seated at the table toward the back of the class.

Bill was the new spa and salon manager, and was joining the Kauwela Resorts team with a unique background. He'd spent many years in the United States Army as a medic, and then was a barber who built a successful barbershop and salon franchise, which he'd scaled exponentially, then sold to a notable firm that owned and operated spas, barbershops, and beauty salons across the country. Arthur was a client of Bill's for years, so they'd built a relationship. Arthur, in his charismatic way, was able to talk Bill into coming out of retirement to join the team for just a couple years to get the Kauwela Resorts spa and salon business off the ground.

"I love that," said Arlene. "So then, for the next step, how can we become intentional with our words?"

Sophia, the new executive chef, took this one, as now, more and more people wanted to add their thoughts to the conversation. Sophia had one of those classic "chef personalities," very quiet and reserved until something struck a chord, when she'd speak up, very intentionally, not to mention passionately. She had spent a couple of decades working her way up to the chef ranks, from her education in culinary school to her first food and beverage role in a poolside cabana at a luxury resort in Orlando, to becoming a pastry chef in a prominent New York City convention hotel near Times Square, to growing into her role as a sous-chef to not one but two celebrity chefs in Manhattan's famed Hell's Kitchen along "restaurant row" on West 46th Street between 8th and 9th, and now finally as an executive chef back to her roots at a well-known, respected hotel brand, Kauwela Resorts.

Like most chefs, she had a very strong personality, as over the years she had to grow thick skin. On the inside, she had a heart of gold, with so much love for people—guests and her own teams—and of course an undeniable, endless love and appreciation for all things food. Summer Grace and her new colleagues were now leaning in, turning completely around in their respective chairs listening and watching Chef Sophia as if it were an episode of *Top Chef*.

"I'm not sure if anyone grew up with this same sentiment, but here goes—something to remember in any situation is *if you can't say anything nice, it's best to simply not say anything at all*. When we're intentional with our words, we only say what needs to be said. We make sure our words are positive, nice, respectful, and kind to other people around us. Our energy will rub off on other people. So, we want our energy to be 'good energy.'" Chef Sophia had everyone captivated.

She continued, "In some of my past roles in high-pressure restaurants, I used to let those high-stress moments get to me. Unfortunately, I got caught up in all the hype that comes from being an up-and-coming high-profile chef, and I said one too many things, with just a little too much arrogance, and it cost me jobs, opportunities, and what was most hurtful of all is that it cost me some of my most treasured relationships. I'm here because I want this to be different, and I want to inspire up-and-coming chefs in the making to be slower to speak, quicker to listen, and slower to anger. Good energy. Positive, upbeat energy will take us all further, quicker, than getting in the jab or the passive-aggressive comment to win the argument or conversations we think we have to win. We can either 'win the argument' or 'win the relationship.' It's a very intentional choice."

Everyone was nodding along. The group was coming together slowly but surely the more they heard each other's thoughts.

With every little anecdote or thought shared, the group of newly hired leaders were starting to get to know one another on a personal level. Arlene and Nick knew exactly what they were doing!

Arlene continued, "The question we like to always ask ourselves around here is: How can we be intentional with our actions, on a consistent basis? Because we know that when positive actions align with our positive thoughts, we create caring environments in which, more often than not, we show compassion to one another and our guests. Being intentional means to stay focused on *making progress*. That means intentional actions either help somebody else get closer to their goal or they help us get closer to achieving our own goal. Since we're the leaders, everyone is watching us. When we're intentional, others not only see it, but they also feel it in the types of environments we create. Let's do an activity to bring this idea of *intentionality* to life."

Arlene explained the activity, and everyone dove into their interactive Participant Guides to write down their thoughts.

"Who would like to share an example of their positive thoughts, words, or actions?" Arlene threw out to the group after she gave them plenty of time to reflect and make some notes.

Summer Grace volunteered and opened up a bit more about why she made the decision to leave her former company and join Kauwela Resorts in the first place.

Intentionality Activity

Setting and Making My Intentions Visible
My three happy thoughts (three things I'm grateful for):
1.
2.
3.

Three nice things I'll say to a coworker:
1.
2.
3.

Three things I will do to show a coworker that I want the best for them (things I will do to help someone make progress toward their goals):

1.

2.

3.

SUMMER GRACE OPENS UP AND SHARES HER STORY

"I've talked to some of you about why I'm here, but others may not know about the toxicity that existed in my last company. It was so toxic that my thoughts were consumed with negativity about my boss and the entire situation, especially toward the end of the experience. So, I'm choosing positivity here, in this experience. While it's already started off in a much more positive direction, I want to make sure I do my part in being intentional about my thoughts, words, and, most importantly, my actions. So, I wrote down three nice things I will share with Arthur, our general manager, whom I'm sure all of you love and respect as much as I do. I'm going to send him a note later this evening recapping how welcome and comfortable I felt when I experienced the restaurant, the pool, and the special touches the housekeeping team made to my guest room last week in my Week One experience."

"Thank you for sharing that, Summer Grace," Arlene said as she invited everyone to give Summer Grace a nice round of applause.

Arlene wrapped up the intentionality section before sending everyone to lunch, "Being *intentional* will always help you stay positive so that you can ultimately Give Compassion, Encouragement, Kindness, and Hospitality to others in your life—friends, teammates, and family. You'll remain grateful for what you have in your life instead of what you do not. That alone will help you stay upbeat, in a great mood, and able to help other people when they need you as their friend."

After a very intentional applause, the group migrated once again to the Gracious Café for lunch. Summer Grace noticed how those cliques from Day One had all of a sudden morphed into one, collective wolf pack, as the entire group of newly welcomed Kauwela Resorts leaders walked with purpose to lunch together deep in conversation.

Chapter 24

Values

Nick kicked off the first conversation of the afternoon with a question. "What does the word *value* mean?"

Jud, ever the philosopher and never shy with sharing his thoughts, offered up his definition. "*Value* is how much something is worth, or how important something is."

Nick said, "Thank you, Jud. We can always count on you to jump in on the philosophical questions. Let's talk about your value. Do you have value?"

Jud smiled and said, "Well, of course." And then he paused.

Nick looked around to everyone in the group and then just laughed. As Nick started laughing, everyone else started laughing, including Jud. "Care to elaborate?" Nick asked Jud, sarcastically.

THE *VALUE* CONVERSATION

Jud jumped right back in. "Well, my value and everyone else's value begins with what they do well. We all have strengths, and those natural strengths are ultimately what make up our value to the world, to society, and to our new community here at Kauwela Resorts."

Nick added, "Remember from yesterday that Giving Hospitality is about helping people. When they're sad, we can lift them up. When they're hurt, we can help them feel better. When they're nervous or scared, we can encourage them. Sometimes the easiest way to help other people is to simply understand our own value and what makes us unique and special. Once we understand our own personal *value*, we can pour ourselves into other people to lift them up and perhaps even help them understand their own strengths and personal value."

Arlene took it from there. "What exactly do we mean by these *personal values* Jud is talking about?"

PERSONAL VALUES

Mary, the new learning and development manager, had researched for years the best way to teach the power of values—both personal and organizational—to many audiences from early childhood education to adult learning experiences in corporate America, so she perked up on this topic.

She said, "Personal values are our fundamental beliefs that guide our behavior. Our values guide us in *how we live our lives* and *how we treat other people—and even ourselves*. Personal values motivate every decision we make and action we take. For example, our personal values—how we really want to behave—determine how we think about certain things, what we say in certain situations, and ultimately what we do in certain situations. Understanding our values is the first step to becoming the type of person we want to become."

Now Arlene and Mary were seemingly dancing. Arlene said, "We have a choice in every situation—we can either be a happy, positive influence on our friends, family, coworkers, team members, and guests, or we can be a negative influence. Which do you want to be?"

Mary added, "When we understand ourselves and what's most important to us—our values—we always have a guiding light to follow, so we make a positive impact instead of a negative one."

Nick picked up his Participant Guide as a prop and said, "Let's do an activity."

Arlene gave the instructions. "From the long list of seventy-two words in your Participant Guide, choose ten words that best describe your own beliefs and attitudes about what's important in life. From your list of ten words, you'll then further narrow them down as you choose from that shortened list the four words that best describe your own beliefs and attitudes about life. The choice will be difficult, as you truly *value* all the words, but this is about picking the *values* that are really the most important to you and what type of person you want to become."

Values Activity

Achievement	Challenge	Dependability
Adventure	Commitment	Dignity
Assertiveness	Community	Diversity
Authenticity	Compassion	Effectiveness
Authority	Consistency	Efficiency
Autonomy	Control	Empathy
Awareness	Cooperation	Equality
Balance	Courage	Excellence
Beauty	Creativity	Fairness
Belonging	Curiosity	Faith
Boldness	Decisiveness	Fidelity

Freedom	Joy	Status
Generosity	Justice	Strength
Goodness	Learning	Success
Grace	Legacy	Teamwork
Gratitude	Loyalty	Tolerance
Growth	Openness	Traditionalism
Health	Order	Transformational
Honesty	Originality	Trust/Trustworthiness
Honor	Peace	Truth-seeking
Hope	Respect	Understanding
Humility	Responsibility	Uniqueness
Independence	Security	Unity
Innovation	Service	Wisdom

My Personal Values and How I'll Bring Them to Life	
Personal values	My specific behaviors to bring them to life
1.	
2.	
3.	
4.	
Kauwela Resorts Values and How I'll Bring Them to Life	
1. Give Compassion	
2. Give Encouragement	
3. Give Kindness	
4. Give Hospitality	
5. Give Leadership	

After everyone spent a good bit of time choosing, narrowing, changing their minds, and re-choosing and re-narrowing down their lists, Arlene asked, "Who would like to share their four values?"

SUMMER GRACE REFLECTS AS EACH PERSON SHARES THEIR PERSONAL VALUES

Summer Grace was as engaged now as she'd ever been in any job. She just sat back and listened as each person in the room shared each of the four personal values they determined during the activity. As each person shared, she couldn't help but notice, once again, the vulnerability and authenticity in each of her new coworkers. While she initially had some anxiety about making the move to Kauwela Resorts, she was feeling more comfortable and at peace with her decision. The more that others shared, the more Summer Grace was compelled to share of herself. Trustworthy bonds were forming with each incremental conversation throughout the week.

Nick brought this segment of the session to a close with some thoughts. "Stay true to your personal values in how you live your life. Let them guide your every thought, word spoken, and action taken. That's why we spent this time discovering your own personal values. When you know and understand who you want to be, you have a built-in guiding light that inspires how you *think*, *speak*, and *act* in every situation in life and, certainly, in your new roles here at Kauwela Resorts. Now that you understand both your *value* and your *values*, you can use them to help other people and yourself."

"Before we dismiss for your final afternoon break of our Hospitality Conversations experience, there are five other *guiding lights* we encourage each of you to keep in mind as you embark on this next chapter of your leadership journey," Arlene announced, sharing some final thoughts on the topic.

She continued, "Without a doubt, your personal values will guide you in continuing to become your absolute best. You also have five additional *values* from which all of us draw inspiration and direction. We've spent the past four days talking in detail about how we can bring each of them to life.

"As you've noticed, our culture here at Kauwela Resorts is rooted in *meaningful conversations with each other about the things that matter*. The things that matter most to us and our guests are our five core values—Compassion, Encouragement, Kindness, Hospitality, and Leadership. With each step we take and with every decision we make, we Give Compassion, we Give Encouragement, we Give Kindness, we Give Hospitality, and we Give Leadership. All the scholars, journalists, business schools, and thought leaders who come to visit us always ask us how we create such an amazing workplace culture and are always taken aback when we tell them it's as simple as that. We simply *give* the best of ourselves, which helps us see and bring out the best in others.

"We choose to live, work, and love through the five-way lens of compassion, encouragement, kindness, hospitality, and leadership. Those are our values."

Summer Grace again reflected on her experience in her last company, working for Derek, who she thought would be a great leader based on all the things he said and promised to her during her interview process and in the many early conversations they shared when she joined his team. As she'd connected with and listened to stories from her new colleagues and all the impactful debrief conversations Arlene and Nick had facilitated, she began to realize why her last organization was so toxic. The executive leadership and even the so-called leaders on every level of that organization were simply all talk and no show. They liked to talk a big game, with their strong company values and game-changing culture. However, in reality, she thought, Derek, the other vice presidents, directors, and even most of the managers rarely "walked their talk." She realized that if Derek and the other leaders around the organization actually lived the illustrious company values they liked to boast about, the experience would have been completely different, and she probably would have never left.

Nick wrapped it up by saying, "And all of you are a part of the family now. Welcome to Kauwela Resorts. Enjoy your break."

Chapter 25

Empathy

Arlene kicked off the final conversation of the week as she'd kicked off many others throughout the experience, asking, "What does *empathy* mean?"

Lee, the new guest services manager, had been trained throughout his whole career on the power of empathy. He spoke right up and said, "Empathy is the ability to understand and actually *feel* what other people are feeling. It means to put yourself in their shoes and it's actually a skill to be able to feel what it must be like experiencing what they are experiencing. I never really understood that empathy was actually a skill until I had a leadership development class with my last company. Working in theme parks and fancy beach resorts on Maui, Oahu, and even in Fiji, I used to get really beat up vocally by very demanding guests when they didn't get their way. I'd go home each night after work resenting them, their hateful words, and even my own bosses for putting me in these seemingly hopeless and oftentimes helpless situations where nothing I could say or do would change how some of these guests felt about how much we or my organization had ruined their trip. My leaders sent a group of us newly promoted customer service supervisors to a one-day leadership training and my mindset was completely transformed. Once I realized that *empathy* was, in fact, a skill which I and others could practice and get better and better at deploying, I found that to be something of a magical anecdote to any irate or problem guest situation. I learned a simple phrase to say, which helped me grow, not only as a leader, but as a human being. It goes like this—'If what happened to you had happened to me or my own family, I'd be just as frustrated as you are right now.' I found that simple, yet profound statement, when delivered genuinely to anyone, be it an upset guest or even an upset or frustrated teammate or coworker, brings down the temperature of an otherwise heated moment. It also opens up the gateway to personal, human connection, which seems to always work like a charm in those situations to positively change the way people feel about us, our brand, or our ability to meet their needs."

Nick loved that response. With a smile and his patented clap, he said, "Couldn't have said it better myself. If we are going to be a community of people who set out each day to help others with our compassion, encouragement, kindness, old-fashioned hospitality, and inspirational leadership, we have to first *understand* how others—whether it be our peers, the teams we lead, our own leaders, or especially our guests—feel before we can help them."

Arlene took the baton and asked, "How can *empathy* help us Give Leadership to each other, our teams, our guests, and even our own leaders as we *manage up* from time to time?"

JUD SHARES MORE KNOWLEDGE

Jud couldn't help himself, as he had taught several courses and had led so many workshops on emotional intelligence over the years.

He said, "Many believe empathy is to care for others. Some

believe empathy is to have sympathy for others. However, empathy is not *caring*, although in order to deploy empathy, we must care about others. Sympathy is feeling sorry for others. Empathy is one step further toward human connection. It's the ability to understand, as Lee described—taking mental and physical steps to genuinely understand—what other people are thinking and feeling. Empathy is the one skill that is intricately woven in, out, and through each component of emotional intelligence.

"Before we can master the art and science of leading others, we must master the art and science of leading ourselves. Empathy is a skill, and it's one that we can all improve upon over time. Without human connection and achieving understanding with and among those we lead, we'll have very little influence, and few will be open to our attempts at inspirational leadership. However, when we deploy empathy with a healthy side of compassion, caring about other people's feelings, situations, and predicaments, everything changes."

Donnie piped back up and said, "I'm still lost. What does empathy have to do with leadership again?"

SUMMER GRACE AND DONNIE RECONNECT ONCE AGAIN ON THE TOPIC OF EMPATHY

Summer Grace was tracking with everything Jud unpacked. So she responded to Donnie, which had become one of her favorite things to do throughout this whole experience.

She said, "Jud, correct me if I'm wrong, but if we want to connect with and inspire people on our teams, understanding how other people feel in certain situations helps us craft our own messaging—such as email, verbal communication, meeting agendas, daily huddles or briefings—so that we continue to move the organization forward in a positive direction, creating a positive atmosphere in the process.

Empathy also allows us to take appropriate action while taking others' feelings and perspectives into account as we make decisions and lead our teams toward progress. Is that right?"

EMPATHY, THE MOST IMPORTANT AND CRITICAL LEADERSHIP SKILL OF ALL

Jud responded, "Absolutely. It sounds super simple, but empathy is quite possibly the most important and critical leadership skill, yet it's also the skill leaders and aspiring leaders most often forget. Leadership is not about us. It's not about what we're able to do, what we say to win the argument, or whether we 'win' every single conversation. The goal and objective of leadership is to *move people to move*. Our role, as leaders, is to first connect with people and then inspire them to do more, become more, and ultimately deliver more of what the organization needs to achieve results. Recall our human behavior conversation earlier. Unless or until leaders connect with people on an emotional, human level, they will rarely inspire anyone to move. Showing empathy is the quickest and surest way to connect with people on a personal, human level, just as Lee shared moments ago. Emotions drive people's decisions to change behavior, and emotion provides the energy for people to move and act in the first place. So, for leaders, it's all about piquing the right emotions that propel people into motion, into action, and into the behavior change needed to deliver results. Simply put, this is what it means to *Lead with Hospitality*. When I learned about that simple phrase and the Kauwela Resorts leadership culture rooted in it, that's when I knew this was the right organization for me."

"Thank you again, Jud. We're so lucky and grateful to have you now as part of our Kauwela Resorts family. Let's do an activity," Arlene said as she prepped the group for one of their final activities.

EMOTIONALLY CONNECTED
PARTNER ACTIVITY

Nick gave the instructions. "Everyone, please partner up with someone with whom you have not partnered, and someone who works in a department different from your own. Take three minutes and tell your partner about a situation going on right now at work or in your life that is keeping you up at night—something causing you stress, discomfort, worry, doubt, or even fear. Your partner will then practice listening to understand, not necessarily listening to respond or solve the issue. The objective of the exercise is to simply listen to understand how they are feeling about the situation. Take three minutes each, explaining your situations keeping you up at night. As your partner is explaining, practice listening and empathizing, putting yourself in their shoes. You have a chart in your Participant Guide with spaces to write down some notes as you're listening with empathy to your partner."

Seeking to Understand with Empathy	
My coworker or partner at work:	
The situation:	
The **Emotions** they're feeling:	
If I were in their **Situation, I** would *Feel*:	

The 20 leaders, who now felt like they knew each other on a more personal level, partnered up and further connected with this conversation. As each person shared a bit more of themselves, partners learned who their partner was on the inside. Arlene and Nick circulated throughout the room, listening and observing along the way. With a look toward each other, they expressed how touched they were by what they were witnessing. Twenty people who had walked into the Aloha Conference Room as individuals had transformed into a connected team, a community of leaders inspired to give the best of themselves while intentionally bringing out the best in others.

ARLENE OFFERS SOME CLOSING THOUGHTS ON EMPATHY

Arlene congratulated and thanked the group for their conscientious approach to each activity and conversation all week long. She offered some final thoughts around empathy.

She said, "Each of us can be shining beacons of positive light for our friends, family members, team members, our leaders, and, as always, especially our guests, as long as we make the choice to do so. Just as you've experienced here today, you can do the same thing in your life outside of work and as a leader here at Kauwela Resorts when you seek to understand how someone else feels. You'll find it in your heart to *give* a little bit of yourself—your time, your strengths, and your care for others—to help them feel better, be better, and ultimately become their absolute best. They will feel better and, in turn, so will you."

ARLENE, NICK, AND ARTHUR CHARISMATICALLY CONCLUDE WEEK TWO

Nick and Arlene took their places in the front of the room in somewhat of a crescendo of emotions, learning, sharing, and meaning all wrapped up in Hospitality Conversations throughout the week. At that moment, in walked Arthur with his charismatic presence that seemed to always captivate everyone's attention.

Arthur engaged the 20 new leaders who would now embark on their journeys as the next generation of Kauwela Resorts leaders one last time for the week. "My new friends, thank you so very much for your time, your special talents, and, most importantly, the heart and soul you've committed to giving to our cause here at Kauwela Resorts. By now I'm sure it's apparent that our focus on *how* we do what we do is almost more important than *what* we do or even where we're going as an organization." Everyone was sitting upright, heads and hearts fixated on Arthur's every word.

Summer Grace, as dialed in as she'd been all week, noticed for the final time the "ALOHA" image, with the words and meanings finally filled all the way in, on the screen:

> **A** – *Akahai* – meaning "**Kindness**" (grace), to be expressed with tenderness.
>
> **L** – *Lokahi* – meaning "unity" (unbroken), to be expressed with harmony and **Compassion**.
>
> **O** – *'Olu'olu* – meaning "agreeable" (gentle), to be expressed with *friendly* **Encouragement**.
>
> **H** – *Ha'aha'a* – meaning "humility" (gentle), to be expressed with **Hospitality**.
>
> **A** – *Ahonui* – meaning "patience" (waiting for the moment), to be expressed with **Leadership**.

Arthur charismatically pointed to the "ALOHA" image with those magical words, which now meant more than just a simple greeting to everyone in the room. He asked the group with a smile and a laugh, "Did anyone notice this image each day as you were all migrating to see Pua at the lobby bar?"

Everyone laughed.

"I actually did notice that each day," Summer Grace said, determined to ask why they didn't cover each of these in order. "I wondered each evening why our conversations weren't linear. Why didn't we talk about them in order?"

Arthur, with a wink and smile to Arlene and Nick, responded gracefully. "Well, Summer Grace, I'm glad you asked that question. The *Spirit of Aloha* is so powerful because to us it's not linear. Instead, it's vertical. Rather than get caught up in the worry and fear of the unknown about what's going to happen next, what we want for all of you and all of our guests is to simply be present in the *now*.

"In the Hawaiian culture, it's known as *embracing the Pa'a*. It's about living free from limiting beliefs, which often come from our own fixed, negative mindsets. If we're not careful, we can limit ourselves from having the levels of joy, fulfillment, and happiness we'd experience with a more positive growth mindset of possibility. So, be free! Live the *Spirit of Aloha* and give the best of yourselves, and when you do—when we all do that together—we'll bring out the best in everyone around us—coworkers, leaders, friends, family, and especially our guests.

"When you come to work each day, don't think of our core values as linear, but instead live them vertically with a constant connection to a Higher Self we're all on a journey to becoming. Give Kindness, Give Compassion, Give Encouragement, Give Hospitality, and Give Leadership early and often. These are truly the things that matter, which bring out the best in all of us."

DO THE LITTLE THINGS. PLAY THE LONG GAME. MAKE A BIG IMPACT.

Arthur continued, "This week was all about immersing you in the *how* with very simple, yet profoundly impactful, Hospitality Conversations about the things that matter most. The secret to our success up to this point, and the secret to *how* we will continue to make progress as an organization, really is that there are no secrets.

"It's less about any one, magical, game-changing thing. Instead, it's hundreds of 'little things.' It's simply about having consistent, meaningful conversations about the things that matter. And as you've just experienced, when we make it all about someone else—each other, our guests, our communities—living, working, and loving from a place of generosity, we continue to *give* the best of ourselves while seeing and bringing out the best in others. Do the little things. Play the long game. And you'll make a big impact. Welcome to the team."

Everyone jumped to their feet and gave a collective, heartfelt round of applause for the final time, closing out their Hospitality Conversations experience. Hugs, high fives, and handshakes filled the room as every single person felt the magic of their newfound community.

Summer Grace had one final question. She'd meant to ask this as soon as she arrived the week prior, but with all the goings-on, it had slipped her mind. She went over to Arthur, Arlene, and Nick, who were exchanging heartfelt hugs of their own with one another.

"Excuse me, Arthur," Summer Grace said, politely entering their circle of hugs. "I've been meaning to ask, what does *Kauwela* mean?"

Arthur glanced quickly at both Arlene and Nick with the widest grin Summer Grace had seen yet, and he said, "I've been waiting for you to ask that question. *Kauwela* means 'summertime' in Hawaiian."

Summer Grace's intuition since accepting Arthur's invitation to join the team was that this really was where she was supposed to be at this point in her life and career. When she found out Kauwela meant "summertime," she was truly moved. Tears began streaming down her cheeks with her genuine smile lighting up the room yet again.

In that moment she realized everything that was supposed to happen had happened, and everything she'd been through up to that point had been purposeful primers preparing her for what would come next as part of a grander plan. She knew that every rough season and tough conversation, along with every triumph, from childhood through her adolescent years and up to that very day as an adult, had prepared her for this moment. She realized that even with a little nervousness and anxiety about starting a new job with a new company, this experience would be yet another *purposeful primer* for more and more growth—personally and professionally—on her journey to becoming who she was destined to become.

Summer Grace was filled up with passion, purpose, and visions of what could be possible *Leading with Hospitality* at Kauwela Resorts. She couldn't wait to meet her new team and continue engaging in conversations about the things that matter with the *Spirit of Aloha* as her guiding light.

It truly was her time.

Summertime.

Epilogue

A Message from Taylor Scott

While this was a fictional story, my hope is that we can all see a little bit of ourselves in Summer Grace and her new colleagues at Kauwela Resorts. From the disappointment that comes with working in toxic workplace cultures, to the nervous anticipation mixed with excitement when we start a new job or project, to the heartfelt compassion and encouragement we receive from our peers—these are all real emotions everyone experiences. You experience them. I experience them. Every person on our teams, in our organizations, and even our guests, customers, and clients experience them. Every day.

The world today is much different and more divided than the world that was. I wrote this story of hope to inspire myself and others to live, work, and love from a place of generosity, to create a more united, compassionate world than we've experienced in recent years.

Give Hospitality is inspired by my 20 years working as a leader in the hospitality and entertainment industries in Central Florida,

Southern California, and Las Vegas; by my favorite teachers, professors, pastors, and coaches; by some of the most generous, loving people I've met and had the privilege to work with and for; by my own family; and by the beauty of the Aloha Spirit.

In 2020, I lost my job and applied to over 150 jobs in the hospitality industry, and in return I received over 150 rejection emails "regretting to inform me" that I would not be moving forward in the hiring process. I was heartbroken, and it was awful. But I was more heartbroken when I'd connect with former coworkers, colleagues, and even some of my closest friends who were also in the same boat. Many hospitality industry workers, leaders, organizations, and wonderful, caring human beings were going through possibly the toughest season anyone had ever faced, professionally or personally. Other industries also found themselves navigating some of the toughest months and years they'd ever experienced as well.

More heartbreaking than that was what was happening in our country and in our divided world. It felt so divided politically, socially, economically, and even emotionally.

To escape it all, I started writing, and dreaming, and thinking, and hoping for a brighter, more joyful season.

SUMMERTIME

Since a summer internship in 1999 in the Walt Disney World College Program, I've dreamed of creating a resort brand called *Summertime Resorts*. I've loved summertime for as long as I can remember. Vacations. Basketball camps. Little League baseball. Pools. Beaches. Palm trees. I've just always loved summertime. So, my dream was and still is to create a place where people could escape their day-to-day and reconnect emotionally with who and what matters most in their lives. So, I wrote a story about what it would be like to not only visit a place like that, but to work at a place like that.

MEET ARTHUR

The general manager in the story, Arthur, is inspired by Arthur Keith, a hospitality industry veteran and my mentor, friend, and colleague since we met in 2007. He's an actual longtime hotel general manager and is currently the general manager of The Statler Hotel at Cornell University.

Arthur has been a mentor to me since I was in graduate school at Cornell University's Nolan School of Hotel Administration. Throughout the many years leading up to that season in 2007, Arthur had spent 30 years rising to the executive leadership ranks in the hospitality industry in Dallas, Orlando, Nashville, and Las Vegas, to name a few of the destinations he's called home.

Two years after graduate school in 2010, I was in a season of transition, having a difficult time finding a job. At the time, Arthur was opening The Cosmopolitan of Las Vegas as the general manager, so I stepped out in *vulnerability* and emailed him to see if he remembered me from three years prior when we met at a Leadership Development Weekend at Cornell. He was generous with his time, his talent, and his resources, and introduced me to the talent acquisition team. Several interviews later, I found myself on the opening team as the director of membership, leading the loyalty marketing team for the next four years. That experience changed me and shaped me in too many ways to count, and it never would have happened if not for Arthur's heart for hospitality and generosity.

Since the summer of 2021, I visit Cornell every few months to give back to the school and to Arthur's mission at The Statler Hotel. I give my time and our Lead with Hospitality leadership development content to the leadership team, student leaders, and even frontline teams at The Statler Hotel at Cornell University. Students in the Hotel Leadership Development Program at The Statler Hotel at Cornell University receive copies of my book *Lead with Hospitality: Be Human. Emotionally Connect. Serve Selflessly.* every single year.

They'll soon receive copies of *Give Hospitality* as well.

LOVE FOR MAUI

In August of 2023, devastating wildfires decimated the city of Lahaina on Maui, in the Hawaiian Islands. An estimated 2,200 buildings were destroyed, including thousands of homes. One hundred people lost their lives in what turned out to be one of the highest death tolls attributed to a US wildfire in over a hundred years.

My wife and I honeymooned in Maui in 2016, and we've been back several times since. We absolutely love everything about it, its people, its culture, its history, and those picturesque views. For me, the experiences at resorts on Maui are everything I've ever dreamed Summertime Resorts could or would ever be.

We visited in November of 2023, as soon as tourists were encouraged to visit once again after the fires, to help accelerate the rebuilding efforts. While on that trip, we purposely took extra cash to tip every bartender, housekeeper, server, front desk agent, valet, bell person, rideshare driver, and gift shop host or hostess to simply *give* to the people who had lost homes, businesses, and family members. While we were on the trip, it was visibly apparent that many had begun to lose hope.

I left Maui inspired to give more to the cause.

I'd written most of this story prior to that visit, but it was on that trip when I decided to make this a purposeful story to inspire generosity in the hearts and minds of as many of us as possible to give or donate to the rebuilding efforts in Maui's beloved harbor town of Lahaina.

So, that's why I named the organization where Summer Grace found hope *Kauwela Resorts*. (*Kauwela*, as you now know, means "summertime" in Hawaiian.)

THE NINTH ISLAND

My wife and I live in Henderson, Nevada, eleven miles from the Las Vegas Strip. Many people call it "the Ninth Island" because so many Hawaiian people live, work, and vacation here. From a young age, and even when I worked for the Walt Disney Company, I always had one eye toward Las Vegas. I've been fascinated with it all my life and I always wanted to learn how they create these memorable, extravagant experiences so consistently. My wife and I chose to live in the Las Vegas area because of the hospitality-centric nature of the destination. Since living here, we've worked with and learned so much from Hawaiian people, their culture, their stories, and, most of all, the magic of *Aloha*.

My hope is that the *Give Hospitality* story not only inspires more selfless generosity in the world, but also compels us to give of ourselves to help rebuild Maui's Lahaina Town so the world will continue to *feel* and *experience* the *Aloha Spirit* that community and its loving, hospitable people have given to the rest of us so generously for decades.

GIVE TO MAUI RELIEF EFFORTS

Hawai'i Community Foundation's *Maui Strong Fund*: https://www.hawaiicommunityfoundation.org

GIVE TO HURRICANE RELIEF EFFORTS

https://www.redcross.org/donate/donation.html/

BOOK YOUR DREAM VACATION TO HAWAII OR ELSEWHERE

Visit us at Lead with Hospitality Travel Group, a Dream Vacations franchise—to research your next "dream vacation" to Hawaii or wherever your dreams take you. Our website is www.LeadWithHospitality TravelGroup.com.

As part of our collective cause, at Lead with Hospitality, LLC, we're not only committed to connecting with, serving, engaging, and inspiring leadership and frontline teams in the hospitality and entertainment industries, but we're also committed to enabling more and more travelers, families, and visitors to experience the *magic of hospitality*. So, we have our own travel agency franchise so that we can send our family, friends, colleagues, partners, and as many people as possible to experience generous hospitality across the world. Visit us at www.LeadWithHospitalityTravelGroup.com or https://tscott.dreamvacations.com. We'd be honored to help you plan your dream vacation.

CREATING KAUWELA RESORTS IN REAL LIFE

If you or someone you know is interested in creating a place where the Spirit of Aloha is felt in every experience, where leaders Lead with Hospitality, where teams deliver memorable hospitality, and where guests reconnect with whom and what matters most in life, I'd love to connect. Reach me at taylor@LeadWithHospitality.com.

I'm currently engaging prospective partners, collaborators, and investors to create the Kauwela Resorts brand in real life.

LEAD WITH HOSPITALITY, LLC

Live Learning Experiences for Leadership Teams and Frontline Teams

Our company, Lead with Hospitality, LLC, creates, designs, and delivers leadership development experiences for leaders at all levels of companies, universities, and community organizations worldwide. We also create, design, and deliver culture cultivating experiences just like Summer Grace and her new colleagues experienced in their first two weeks on the job at Kauwela Resorts.

Everything Lead with Hospitality, LLC does is on purpose, with a purpose, for a purpose to *connect, serve, engage,* and *inspire* leaders and teams to transform *jobs* into truly *meaningful work* with our *Edutainment* style of facilitating memorable and inspiring learning experiences.

Visit us at www.LeadWithHospitality.com.

We look forward to the connection, conversations, and collaboration. Aloha.

Taylor Scott
Founder and President
Lead with Hospitality, LLC

ACKNOWLEDGMENTS

I first wrote this "story" just three months after the team at Matt Holt Books and I launched our most recent book, *Lead with Hospitality*, in April of 2021. When I sent it to Matt Holt, he was generous with his time and his feedback. He simply said at the time, "It's not a no. It's not yet." We needed to GIVE *Lead with Hospitality* more time in the marketplace, and I realized that I needed to GIVE myself time to not only grow myself but to also grow our Lead with Hospitality, LLC business, our reach, and our ability to inspire positive change, together.

Thank you to Matt Holt and the team at BenBella Books for not only answering my many phone calls and emails, but also for your gracious and generous hospitality in the time, effort, energy, and care you've given to me, our team, and this *Hospitality movement* we've set out to inspire. Thank you for your partnership in bringing the story of Summer Grace and Kauwela Resorts to life and ultimately *giving* it to the world at the right time, for the right purpose. To Mallory Hyde, Lydia Choi, Katie Dickman, Brigid Pearson, Adrienne Lang, Ariel Jewett, Raquel Moreno, and Matt Holt, thank you for your partnership to bring this story to life.

In 2010, in the midst of the financial crisis, many of us in the hospitality industry were struggling to find work. I sent an email to Arthur

Keith, whom I'd met during my time in graduate school at Cornell University. As a Cornell alum, he had returned to campus to GIVE his time, talent, and his own resources to us, the up-and-comers about to graduate from the Nolan School of Hotel Administration's Masters of Management in Hospitality program. Thank you to Arthur, not only for your generosity back then, giving me a chance to return to Las Vegas for what became a life- and career-changing experience as part of the opening team of The Cosmopolitan of Las Vegas, but also for your mentorship, friendship, and professional partnership over the years. Your generosity and heart for hospitality inspired me to write this story about the magic of both *generosity* and *hospitality*. In your role today, as the general manager of The Statler Hotel at Cornell University, it's a beautiful thing to work alongside you. You're still GIVING your time, talent, and resources to the up-and-comers, the students at the Cornell Nolan School of Hotel Administration, the leaders and teams at The Statler Hotel, and to the Ithaca, New York, community we all love and cherish.

Thank you to the Cornell Nolan School of Hotel Administration students, faculty, staff, and the leadership and frontline teams of The Statler Hotel at Cornell University. Being your partner in all things leadership and learning since the summer of 2021 has been and continues to be the most meaningful work I've ever been blessed to do. I love you, and I will forever intend to GIVE my time, talent, and heart to our collective Cornell University mission to "do the greatest good."

To my former leaders and coworkers at the Walt Disney Company, Gaylord Hotels and Resorts, Wynn Resorts, and The Cosmopolitan of Las Vegas, it wasn't always beautiful, but what a beautiful ride it was and has been. I am forever grateful for the opportunity to work, dream, envision, create, inspire, and lead alongside and within each of your organizations. From an early age, all I've ever wanted to do was to live and work in and around the magical hospitality destinations, products, and experiences that you've always created for all of us. Thank you for the inspiration for this story and so much more.

To our Lead with Hospitality, LLC clients, client organizations, and partners—United Airlines, Choice Hotels, Highgate Hotels, Sodexo Live!, Jones Lang LaSalle, Fidelity Investments, The Statler Hotel at Cornell University, and Montage Hotels and Resorts, to name a few—thank you for the trust you've put into us and our ability to be your partner in all things leadership and learning across each of your organizations over the years. Each of your brands has been and continues to be an inspiration for the work we do as an organization as well as how I strive to live my own life, with a heart for hospitality.

Thank you to our Lead with Hospitality, LLC team. From the beginning we all set out to co-create a community of like-minded leaders, facilitators, dreamers, creators, and deliverers of *Edutainment Experiences* for each other and especially for our clients. Working with each of you these past several years has been an honor and a privilege. Thank you for answering those phone calls and emails when all of this was (and in many ways still is) but a vision of many stories worth telling about the many inspiring experiences we could create and deliver for people, all in the spirit of generous hospitality. I look forward to many more experiences about which we can share more stories for years to come. This is work worth doing, and it's certainly an honor to do it all with you,

Thank you to my mom and dad (Mary, the new training manager, and Jeff, the new corporate attorney, in the story) for putting vacation after vacation on credit cards only to book the next vacation before paying off the last. Thank you for the lessons in leadership and life you have taught and continue to teach me and so many others. Thank you for all the deep breaths, love, and compassion you continue to GIVE me each time I tell you another idea for the next book, business, or dream vacation on the horizon. It's the experiences we've all shared on vacations, long weekends, and even in each of our homes over the years that continue to inspire me to inspire others with more stories and learning experiences. I love you and I look forward to welcoming you to Kauwela Resorts one day.

Finally, thank you to my beautiful inside and out wife, Jenna, for the hours upon hours of idea sharing, conversations, dreaming, traveling, and listening over the years. When I've been in between jobs or out of a job, your generosity, love, and hospitality have kept me hopeful, energized, and inspired to keep going. Everything I do in my work today, whether writing or speaking, building business, or traveling in search of the next book or story, always has, and always will be, to GIVE you the life you deserve. I love you, and I can't wait until our next flight together to Maui. Let's splurge, and book first class.

ABOUT THE AUTHOR

Taylor Scott is a best-selling author, inspirational keynote speaker, and leadership development consultant.

His books, leadership development programs, and keynotes are inspired by a 20-year leadership career in the hospitality and entertainment industries, working for Disney Parks and Resorts, Gaylord Hotels and Resorts, Wynn Resorts, and The Cosmopolitan of Las Vegas.

Taylor is the author of *Ballgames to Boardrooms: Leadership, Business, and Life Lessons from Our Coaches We Never Knew We Needed* and *Lead with Hospitality: Be Human. Emotionally Connect. Serve Selflessly*, published by Matt Holt Books, an imprint of BenBella Books, in 2021.

Taylor lives in Henderson, NV, with his beautiful wife, Jenna. They enjoy working out, traveling, shopping, dining, and visiting as many hotel lobby bars as possible.

A sample of Taylor's clients and partners:

- United Airlines
- Jones Lang Lasalle
- The Statler Hotel at Cornell University
- Highgate Hotels
- Alamo Drafthouse
- Choice Hotels
- Montage Resorts
- Fidelity Investments
- Sodexo Live!
- Breeze Airways
- Sesame Collective
- Dartmouth Health

CONNECT WITH US

We invite you to experience more conversations, collaboration, and connection with our Lead with Hospitality, LLC. Team and Taylor Scott.

TAYLOR SCOTT KEYNOTES

Keynotes customized to engage your leaders and teams.
https://leadwithhospitality.com/william-taylor-scott/

Bring EDUTAINMENT! to Your Organization

Live Learning Experiences by
Lead with Hospitality, LLC

Learning Experiences designed to serve your leaders, frontline team members, and facilitators.
https://leadwithhospitality.com/work-with-us/

COMPLIMENTARY RESOURCES

We invite you to join our weekly newsletter or share our action plans with your team. They will help you keep the messages throughout this book at the forefront of your leadership journey.
https://leadwithhospitality.com/resources/

Taylor Scott
taylor@LeadWithHospitality.com
www.LeadWithHospitality.com
www.LeadWithHospitalityTravelGroup.com
321-297-6323

EXPERIENCE HOSPITALITY

LEAD WITH HOSPITALITY TRAVEL GROUP BY DREAM VACATIONS

We've set out to make a positive impact on our most beloved hospitality industry brands and destinations by connecting with and sending as many incremental guests, customers, and clients as possible to our favorite places and experiences.

We're on a mission to connect people to the moments that matter most by helping our friends, colleagues, partners, and fellow travelers plan and book dream vacations to Disney Parks and Resorts, Disney Cruises, Hawaii, Las Vegas, Southern California, and some of the most exclusive and value-added cruises with Royal Caribbean, Celebrity Cruises, Norwegian Cruise Line, to name a few, and land packages you'll find anywhere in the industry.

LOVE FOR HAWAII

A portion of the proceeds of this book will be donated to the Maui Strong Fund. Join us in GIVING Love and Hospitality:
https://www.hawaiicommunityfoundation.org/give

Another way to help the families, local businesses, and hospitality industry professionals who lost everything in the Maui wildfires is to visit Maui as the community continues to rebuild.

We're excited to share our passion and love for Hawaii.

Visit us at www.LeadWithHospitalityTravelGroup.com to explore some of the amazing vacation experiences we can help you dream, plan, book, and experience!